DE LUBAC

Guides for the Perplexed available from Continuum:

DE LUBAC: A GUIDE FOR THE PERPLEXED

DAVID GRUMETT

With a foreword by
Avery Cardinal Dulles

t & t clark

Published by T&T Clark
A Continuum imprint
The Tower Building, 11 York Road, London SE1 7NX
80 Maiden Lane, Suite 704, New York, NY 10038

www.continuumbooks.com

British Library Cataloguing-in-Publication Data
A catalogue record for this book is available from the British Library.

ISBN-10: HB: 0-8264-9314-9
PB: 0-8264-9315-7
ISBN-13: HB: 978-0-8264-9314-9
PB: 978-0-8264-9315-6

Typeset by Servis Filmsetting Ltd, Manchester
Printed on acid-free paper in Great Britain by
Athenaeum Press Ltd, Gateshead, Tyne and Wear

CONTENTS

FOREWORD

by Avery Cardinal Dulles, S.J.

In retrospect the twentieth century will perhaps be seen as one of the great ages of Christian theology. It rivals the fifth, the thirteenth, and the sixteenth centuries for having produced authors of erudition, creativity, and eloquence. Among Protestants, the names of Karl Barth, Rudolf Bultmann, and Paul Tillich stand out, even though critics will variously assess the value of their contributions. On the Catholic side, Karl Rahner, Yves Congar, and Hans Urs von Balthasar are outstanding, and Henri de Lubac surely belongs to this stellar group. Amid difficult circumstances he managed to achieve an extraordinary mastery of the Greek and Latin Fathers, the monastic tradition, and the Baroque period. Though primarily a historical theologian, he played an influential part in many inner-Catholic discussions of his day.

De Lubac never believed that theology could be pursued in isolation from current trends, whether ecclesiastical or secular. During the Second World War he was passionately engaged in the French underground, working against the Vichy government, particularly because of its complicity in the anti-Semitism of the Nazis. Exploring the roots of modern atheism, he brilliantly analysed the rise of secularism, as exemplified by Ludwig Feuerbach, Karl Marx, and Auguste Comte. He also wrote a careful booklength study of the socialist Pierre-Joseph Proudhon.

In his personal thought de Lubac was deeply influenced by several immediate predecessors: the French Jesuit Pierre Rousselot, the Belgian Jesuit Joseph Maréchal, and the French layman Maurice Blondel. Under their influence he promoted a personalist philosophy that sought to integrate some of the best insights of Immanuel Kant into a Thomistic framework. He judged that something had gone seriously awry with the scholastic tradition in the sixteenth and seventeenth centuries, with Tommaso de Vio Cajetan, Francisco Suárez, and their successors. He sharply criticized the neo-scholastics of his own day, both Jesuit and Dominican, and they in turn judged his work novel and dangerous.

During the 1950s de Lubac and his associates were accused of promoting a new theology (*nouvelle théologie*) – a term that displeased de Lubac, as readers of the present work will learn. Highly placed Roman prelates shared in the suspicion. They understood him as holding that God could have created human beings with a purely natural end. Pope Pius XII was thought to have condemned that view when, in the encyclical *Humani generis* (1950), he referred to some who undermine the special gratuity of the supernatural order. Also suspect were de Lubac's views on the Eucharist. His willingness to speak of the Eucharist as Christ's 'mystical body', reviving the practice of some early medieval theologians, seemed difficult to reconcile with the doctrine of transubstantiation.

The neo-scholastics were not de Lubac's only adversaries. His promotion of the fourfold sense of Scripture was displeasing to many working exegetes, who preferred to limit themselves to the literal meaning of the text – the meaning that had been intended by its human authors. They considered the spiritual exegesis favoured by de Lubac vague, arbitrary, and even obscurantist.

It may have been providential that the papal nuncio to France in the mid-1950s was Giuseppe Roncalli, the future Pope John XXIII. While in Paris he seems to have gained a deep respect for Henri de Lubac and Yves Congar, both of whom were under suspicion from Rome at the time. Shortly after announcing the convening of the Second Vatican Council, Pope John XXIII appointed them both to take part in the preparations. Like Congar, de Lubac served as a *peritus* (theological consultant) for all four sessions of Vatican II.

The Second Vatican Council seems to bear many traces of de Lubac's influence, notably in what it has to say on Christ as the centre of history, Scripture and tradition, the catholicity of the Church, the Church as sacrament, the theology of missions, religious freedom, the Jews, Buddhism, and Marxist atheism. Even if de Lubac did not intervene on all these questions, his writings prior to the Council greatly influenced the assembled Fathers. At the Council de Lubac found a kindred spirit in Karol Wojtyla, with whom he continued to correspond for some years. At one point he even expressed the hope that Wojtyla might become pope, as happened in 1978. Pope John Paul II reciprocated his esteem and named him a cardinal in 1983.

After the Council Paul VI appointed him one of the original members of the International Theological Commission, where he developed close working relationships with Hans Urs von Balthasar and Joseph Ratzinger, the future Pope Benedict XVI.

Even after his rehabilitation at Vatican II, de Lubac remained controversial. He severely denounced some of the liberal interpretations of the Council, especially those promoted in the Dutch periodical *Concilium*. He was a founding editor of the international review *Communio*, which in many respects served as a conservative counterweight to *Concilium*. During the decade following the Council, he spoke out against what he regarded as the hypertrophy of national and regional episcopal conferences, and denied that they possessed true doctrinal authority. He was critical of the bishops for allowing their policies to be dictated by a bureaucracy of professionals.

Although sometimes called conservative, de Lubac was not typical of that breed. Throughout his career he championed the causes of theologians who had been judged less than orthodox. He did a great deal to rehabilitate the third-century Alexandrian theologian Origen. Toward the end of his career he wrote a very favourable monograph on the Renaissance Platonist Giovanni Pico della Mirandola, who had been in some trouble with Roman authorities. About the time of Vatican II he composed several volumes in defence of the orthodoxy of Pierre Teilhard de Chardin – a task he undertook at the behest of the superior general of the Society of Jesus, who was worried that the works of Teilhard might be condemned as unorthodox.

Altogether, the theological career of Henri de Lubac was a stormy one, marked by triumphs and defeats, successes and failures. Since his death he has gained a growing number of ardent disciples. Rereading his works today, we will do well to keep in mind that they were not composed in a vacuum. He was not a pure systematician, dispassionately working out the logical consequences of ideas. He was emphatically a man of the Church, deeply involved in the pastoral problems of the day. He was also a man of tradition, seeking to retrieve earlier insights that could be of help for our own time. A master of the apt quotation, he often cited the words of others to express his own thoughts. He did so partly out of modesty, no doubt, but also because he believed that good theology stands within the great tradition.

The present book is, to the best of my knowledge, unique at the present time because it surveys the thinking of de Lubac not on one theme or another but on nearly all the major questions he treated. The advantage of this approach is that it shows the comprehensiveness of de Lubac's oeuvre and his consistency. But the informed reader will recognize that he wrote primarily as historical theologian eager to serve the pastoral needs of the Church in his day. He did so with such learning, elegance, and relevance that his words will be treasured for many years to come.

ACKNOWLEDGEMENTS

The sustained engagement with de Lubac's oeuvre which the writing of this book has required has been a joy assisted by several people. Brian Davies, Gavin D'Costa and Paul McPartlan have offered assistance and encouragement at different stages, and Thomas Kraft of Continuum has provided efficient backing since first hearing my idea. Mark Wynn and Douglas Hedley have been supportive as always, and Tom Plant has helped me clarify some ideas. In Paris, Laurent Bourgeade and the brothers of the Couvent Saint-Jacques offered warm hospitality, whilst in London Guy Sawyer, and David Friend, to whom the book is dedicated, did the same.

INTRODUCTION: A THEOLOGICAL LIFE

Henri de Lubac was a Jesuit theologian born on 20 February 1896 who undertook his formation in the aftermath of the First World War. This was a period of intense social and theological ferment for French Jesuits. Along with members of other religious orders, they had been required to fight for their country. Many, including de Lubac, came from conservative provincial families and entered the order aged seventeen. The maelstrom of war expanded irreversibly their intellectual, social and vocational horizons. De Lubac shot and killed in the war and suffered recurring pain in later life from injuries sustained.[1]

In 1902 religious teaching communities had been expelled from France, and de Lubac therefore pursued most of his studies abroad. Following a semester at Hales Place, Canterbury, he arrived on the island of Jersey late in the summer of 1920 to begin his three years of philosophy. The Maison Saint-Louis in St Helier, the Jesuit scholasticate where he was based, delivered a traditional syllabus under the conservative leadership of the rector, Gabriel Picard, and the uncompromising Suárezian, Pédro Descoqs.[2] De Lubac recalls the 'philosophy courses . . . during which I sometimes scribbled some rather nonconformist notes . . . They were inspired more by Saint Thomas than by my Suarezian master, whose combative teaching was a perpetual invitation to react.'[3] Like all Jesuits of his generation, de Lubac thus approached theology via philosophy, which in his case became a *critique* of a particular form of philosophy launched from within philosophy.

After a year working at the Jesuit college at Mongré in the Rhône, de Lubac moved in the late summer of 1924 to Ore Place, overlooking the town of Hastings on the south coast of England, to embark on his four years of theology. The atmosphere was quite different from on Jersey. The groundbreaking journal *Recherches de science religieuse*, launched in 1910, had included in its first two years of publication twenty contributions by no fewer than seven Hastings scholars. Significant foundations were laid in Hastings for the developments commonly known as *nouvelle théologie* by figures like Léonce de Grandmaison the Rector, the Pauline scholar Ferdinand Prat, and Joseph Huby. De Lubac was a member of the Sunday meeting 'La Pensée' in which the first sketch of his major study *Surnaturel* was born. The group met under the patronage of Huby, whom de Lubac states 'had warmly encouraged me to verify whether the doctrine of Saint Thomas on this important point was indeed what was claimed by the Thomist school around the sixteenth century, codified in the seventeenth and asserted with greater emphasis than ever in the twentieth'.[4]

These obscure origins above an English seaside town have been little understood. De Lubac is typically identified as the leader of a movement named *nouvelle théologie*, but at no point did there exist a coherent school comparable with, for instance, the Dominican Le Saulchoir, defined by manifesto and personnel.[5] The ideas which de Lubac and others were addressing possessed, moreover, deep roots back to figures like Pierre Rousselot, a Jesuit killed in battle in the First World War, and the Catholic lay philosopher Maurice Blondel, made famous by his 1893 thesis *L'Action*. Furthermore, de Lubac himself uses the phrase *nouvelle théologie* pejoratively with consistency over a long period of time. When discussing liberal interpretations of the teaching of the Second Vatican Council in 1980 he critically asserts: 'This famous "spirit of the Council", which those who invoke it most have nourished with their own ideologies, is so seductive and so powerful that it soon obliges its adorers to accept a whole "new theology".'[6] As early as 1946, moreover, he refers critically to the separation of philosophy from theology around the sixteenth century as engendering a 'new theology' founded on the concept of pure nature.[7]

Following the appointment of the former rector Jean-Baptiste Costa de Beauregard as new Provincial in June 1926, the decision was taken to relocate the theologate back to Fourvière in Lyons, where de Lubac completed the remaining two years of his theological formation. The teaching of theology by members of religious orders remained strictly illegal until 1940 but was by this time tolerated by the authorities, partly in recognition of the sacrifice which many of them had made for the nation in the First World War. A

year later, de Lubac delivered his first lecture in the Theology
Faculty as Professor of Fundamental Theology.[8] Facilities were
limited. He recalls:

> In September 1929, I arrived on the Lyons peninsula, at the resi-
> dence on the rue d'Auvergne. It was an old shack that was demol-
> ished shortly afterward. In the loft where I was lodged, which was
> lit by a little skylight, I had not a single book. The Fourvière
> library was scarcely accessible: it had no room at that time where
> one could work, and none of the books could be checked out; the
> library of the Catholic Faculties was miserable: two dusty rooms
> in an old, shaky main building with a little bit of everything.
> Fortunately I discovered a treasure in the attic of Saint Joseph's
> day school, in the beautiful, old-fashioned quarters located over
> the chapel: a library, particularly of literature, which had long
> been neglected but which contained several tiers of theology well
> furnished with old books.[9]

De Lubac did not teach in the Jesuit scholasticate at Fourvière, the
hill overlooking the modern city centre from the west, but in the
Catholic Theological Faculty on the central Presqu'île peninsula
surrounded by the River Saône on the western side and the Rhône
on the east. He evokes the convivial atmosphere characteristic of
faculty gatherings: 'The basic essentials of these meetings consisted
of a good meal, followed by good recreation . . . Then, before breaking up, we quickly reviewed the list of students, and, if necessary, the
dean gave a few opinions.'[10] De Lubac had close contact with doc-
toral students. One of those was Hans Urs von Balthasar, who
records the decisive impact of their encounter during the autumn of
1933 on the direction of his studies towards patristic writers like
Gregory of Nyssa, Maximus the Confessor and Origen.[11]

Lack of resources was by no means the only obstacle confronting
de Lubac. The rigid scholasticism against which he had reacted on
Jersey was gaining ground, buttressed by approved reading lists, the
Index of proscribed works, periodic investigations into doctrinal
orthodoxy, and the requirement to submit all theological manuscripts to *réviseurs* for approval prior to publication. He recollects:

> A certain Scholastic conservatism, which claimed in all good faith
> to be tradition itself, was alarmed at any appearance of novelty. A

kind of so-called 'Thomist' dictatorship, which was more a matter of government than intellectuality, strove to stifle any effort toward freer thought. A network made up of several professors and their former students, which was spread throughout the world, distrusted anything that came into existence outside itself.[12]

This scholasticism is what de Lubac primarily means by 'modern theology': a form of theology organized around the philosophical concept of 'pure nature', which supposes separation between nature and the supernatural such that nature is able to attain only purely natural ends.[13] Its proponents, prevented by patronage systems from engaging in serious debate about those philosophical suppositions, he describes less confusingly as 'new Thomists'.[14]

Political pressures of a more disturbing kind increased following the German invasion of the southern zone of France in November 1942, even though the government in Vichy had recently legalized the Jesuits' position. He recalls: 'The tension was constant. We lived in a fever increased by hunger, by the daily horror of the news, by the next day's uncertainty. And yet, work was carried on, becoming even more intense.'[15] Indeed it was the war that offered de Lubac the opportunity to work on the text of his major study *Surnaturel*, from which teaching responsibilities had over the preceding decade distracted him. He explains:

In June 1940, leaving in haste with a group of companions for La Louvesc, after having evaded the Germans who were approaching Lyons, I carried along a bag with a parcel of notes in it, among which was the notebook for *Surnaturel*. I spent several days up there putting a little order into it. Soon there was the return from our exodus . . . and I gave no more thought to it. But when, in 1943, being hunted by the Gestapo, I had to flee once more, I again carried along my notebook. Hidden away in Vals, which I could not leave and where I could not engage in any correspondence, I thus had something to occupy my retreat. Taking advantage of the resources offered by the Vals library, the manuscript swelled. When I came back to Lyons soon after the departure of the German army, it was ready to be delivered to the printer.[16]

Owing to the postwar paper shortage the printing of the work was limited to just 700 copies, and even those produced used low quality paper and binding.[17] The concrete political controversies surrounding the actions of the French Church during this occupation period make careful examination of de Lubac's response to events and assessment of the period especially important. Shortly after his death, for instance, an essay was published in his name criticizing alleged episcopal collaboration. The authorship has since been shown to have been misattributed.[18]

While de Lubac continued work in Lyons, his fellow Jesuit Karl Rahner pursued a somewhat different path across the Alps at the University of Innsbruck. Rahner's supernatural existential was founded on a philosophical conception of human life which supposed that there was an aspect of human nature oriented to accept divine grace and on which God could act. De Lubac's concept of the *surnaturel* granted insufficient space to philosophy and the distinctive quality of divine action in Rahner's opinion, although de Lubac for his part eirenically affirms that Rahner's views 'corresponded rather closely to what I myself was thinking, aside from a mixture of Heideggerian vocabulary that did not seem to me necessary or even opportune in a study of scholastic tradition'.[19] One might well argue that Rahner's theology retains within itself a philosophical conception of pure nature, with the centrality of metaphysical questions and those about knowledge limiting the capacity of theology to establish its own prior discourse about human existence.

De Lubac's adult life encompasses the whole of what Eric Hobsbawm has called the 'short' twentieth century, extending from the First World War to the collapse of the Soviet Union in 1991, the year in which he died. His theological writing covers most of this period. An introduction to de Lubac thus also provides an overview of a large part of twentieth-century French catholic theology. De Lubac frequently draws insights from historical debates highly pertinent to current theology, and his discussion of topics like faith and reason, the Church, and Buddhism contain profound pastoral insights. His ideas exerted formative influence on both Pope Benedict XVI and Archbishop Rowan Williams.

Surprisingly, this is the first English introduction to de Lubac's theology to be written. Hans Urs von Balthasar's *The Theology of Henri de Lubac* is a translation of his brief 1976 German study which omits several key topics (nature and grace, historical theology, political theology), draws contestable conclusions about others (Buddhism, the Eucharist) and takes no account of de Lubac's late work. Two volumes have been produced in the past ten years each dealing with specific aspects of his theology: Paul McPartlan's excellent *The Eucharist Makes the Church: Henri de Lubac and John Zizioulas in Dialogue*, and Susan Wood's *Spiritual Exegesis and the Church in the Theology of Henri de Lubac*. More recently, interest in de Lubac beyond Catholic circles has been generated by John Milbank's *The Suspended Middle: Henri de Lubac and the Debate Concerning the Supernatural*. The study here presented seeks to provide a balanced, contextual and accessible account to help readers understand these various debates as well as to introduce some new ones.

CHAPTER ONE

GOD AND NATURE

In 1879, Pope Leo XIII promulgated the encyclical *Aeterni patris*. His intention was to exhort Catholic theologians throughout the world to reform their teaching and apologetics in accordance with the philosophy of St Thomas Aquinas. The encyclical identified Aquinas's philosophy as specifically 'Christian philosophy', in distinction with that of other major thinkers such as Descartes. Leo wished to reinstate into theology a philosophical method that supported and required belief in Christ as defined by the Church. The encyclical asserted: 'The catholic philosopher will know that he violates at once faith and the laws of reason if he accepts any conclusion which he understands to be opposed to revealed doctrine.' Leo's second justification for commending Aquinas's philosophy was that it synthesized all previous Christian thought. He more than any other theologian had performed the task of 'diligently collecting, and sifting, and storing up, as it were, in one place, for the use and convenience of posterity the rich and fertile harvests of Christian learning scattered abroad in the voluminous works of the holy Fathers'.[1] Official efforts to re-establish not only Aquinas's theology, but a particular interpretation of it, persisted and became increasingly systematic. In 1914, the Sacred Congregation of Studies published the Twenty-Four Theses, propositions summarizing the central tenets of this orthodoxy to be taught in all colleges as fundamental elements of philosophy.

De Lubac wished to challenge the intellectual historiography of *Aeterni patris*. In his view the theologians who preceded Aquinas needed to be read and studied individually and each in their own terms, and their work could not be judged solely on the basis of its conformity with supposed Thomist norms or divergence from them. De Lubac states of Aquinas and the 'Thomism' to which his work gave birth: 'I do not regard the "common Doctor" as an "exclusive Doctor" who dispenses us from the task of familiarizing ourselves with the others; and I deem it regrettable that a certain partiality, inspired by a misguided strictness and artificial controversies, should sometimes have obscured the sense of profound unity which exists among the great masters.'[2] This study of the wider patristic heritage became known as *ressourcement*: the re-resourcing of theology by making possible a return to its original sources. De Lubac's outstanding contribution to this enterprise was his foundation of the *Sources chrétiennes* series in 1940, co-edited with Jean Daniélou. This series, in which over 500 volumes have now been published, consists of patristic texts in their original language accompanied by a parallel French translation. De Lubac believed profoundly in the power of the church fathers to inspire engaged and rigorous theology: 'Every time, in the West, that Christian renewal has flourished, in the order of thought as in that of life . . . it has flourished under the sign of the Fathers.'[3] The twentieth-century patristic renewal to a very large extent made possible, he argues, the *aggiornamento*, or deep renewal of faith, manifested in the Second Vatican Council (1962–5).

De Lubac's method of employing these sources in his own theology has become known as 'historical theology'. This is an approach to theological reasoning which traces the historical development of theological concepts and shifts in their meaning in order to engage with them critically and creatively. The French present historic tense invests these with a sense of peculiar immediacy. Historical theology was de Lubac's response to the attempt to impose a single normative pattern on Catholic theology based on the new interpretation of Thomist philosophy. His assessment of the work of the Renaissance philosopher Pico della Mirandola could fairly be applied to his own: 'A stand for intellectual pluralism against the narrowness of the school. One there senses irritation at totalizing pretensions, even stronger among certain contemporary Thomists, that their system has been making rigid and unfaithful to the spirit of its origins.'[4] De Lubac wished, in contrast with this univocal approach to the writing of theological history, to recover and engage the full breadth of theological tradition preceding Aquinas. This was a valuable exercise both in itself, and for the deeper and more accurate understanding of the Thomist synthesis it made possible.

THE THEORY OF PURE NATURE

De Lubac's critique of the history of modern theology becomes a quest for the origins of a concept of nature, and especially human nature, as complete in itself and not dependent for its preservation on divine action. This concept has been termed *pure nature*. A further piece of terminology needs to be introduced here, with which de Lubac is closely associated: the *supernatural* (*surnaturel*). He states: 'The idea of the supernatural is as essential to Christianity as, for instance, the ideas of creation, revelation, the Church or sacraments.'[5]

The full meaning of this term will become clear in due course, but a brief prior word of clarification is needed. The 'supernatural' does not refer to some kind of mystical religious experience, inexplicable event, or numinous quality of material objects, as the English translation of the word and its popular usage might suggest. De Lubac prefers, in fact, to use the term 'preternatural' to describe these types of events and experiences.[6] It has nothing to do with flying saucers, crop circles or spiritualism. The following excerpt from *Surnaturel*, which de Lubac repeated more than thirty years later in a study summarizing his theology of nature and grace, provides an excellent initial picture of the qualities he has in mind, and those he does *not* have in mind:

> The supernatural is certainly not the abnormal in the sense that a miracle is. Yet it is more marvellous than the miracle, and its achievement lies much farther beyond the powers of our human nature than a miracle surpasses the *powers* of the physical agents found in material nature. Nor is the supernatural something adventitious, something 'superadded' such as may have been the 'supernatural gifts' attributed to humankind while it was still in the state of innocence; yet it 'dignifies' humanity much more than these did; it raises humanity much higher still above the level of its own *essence*, since it is entirely out of proportion with that essence. Finally, the supernatural must not be defined solely by its characteristic of gratuitousness; and yet it is infinitely more gratuitous than any other kind of favour could possibly be, and infinitely surpasses the *necessities* [*exigences*] of any possible nature. In this triple sense it fully deserves its name.[7]

De Lubac notes in his memoirs that the 'supernatural' terminology which needed reviving in the interwar period is too abstract by current theological standards and should be replaced with language referring to the covenant or mystery of Christ.[8] He also acknowledges that it does not fully express the 'reality of the communication that God makes of himself in Jesus Christ'.[9] Even at the time, de Lubac mooted developing a more explicitly Christological focus for his theology by founding a seminar in Lyons, but felt the climate was not right.[10] Nevertheless, it remains useful because it forewarns against the temptation of 'naturalizing the mystery'. The natural–supernatural distinction continues to be fundamental to de Lubac's project, but is nevertheless 'paralleled by a second distinction which completes and specifies it concretely', which is that between nature and grace.[11] This division, as will be seen, allows the concept of God to be developed in a more personal and responsive mode which nonetheless allows proper account to be taken of the differences between God's being and human being.

The idea of 'pure nature' is formulated as part of the ongoing debate about the precise character of the vision of God. In catholic theological tradition, the yearning of humanity for union with God has frequently been described in terms of *vision*. The 'vision of God' is not used in this context to describe a face-to-face encounter of the kind that one human being might have with another.[12] It suggests in contrast a form of human knowledge of God at once intellectual, emotional and sensory, in which the differentiation of human being from divine being is preserved. Two scholastic theologians are key in its development.[13] *Thomas Cajetan* (1468–1534) is important because his commentary on Thomas Aquinas's *Summa theologiae* was published as part of the new official critical edition of the compendium (1888–1906) at the behest of Leo XIII. Cajetan believed that humanity desires the vision of God, but that this desire is not a result of natural inclination, but produced by grace. Although humanity is unable ever to attain the vision of God naturally, he argues, nature 'would not bestow an inclination to something to which the whole power of nature cannot lead'.[14] The desire of human nature for union with God is, therefore, the result of *grace* and not of nature, and will be satisfied only following the conclusion of natural life.

Francisco Suárez (1548–1617) later laid out a systematic definition of Cajetan's insights, and in so doing made more explicit the concept of pure nature implicit in them. The Suárezian variety of Thomism reigned supreme in the Maison Saint-Louis at St Helier on Jersey, where de Lubac had studied philosophy, and his critique of it is a reaction against early exposure. Suárez argued, in particular, that humanity possesses a distinct spiritual nature on which God may elect to act, and proposed a model of pure nature and graced nature which denied the possibility of real interaction between the two. De Lubac summarizes this theory succinctly: 'In the complete system, the two series – pure nature and supernaturalized nature, or nature called to the supernatural – flowed along parallel channels in complete harmony.'[15] The description of nature as 'pure' suggests that it exists independently of divine action, and can be understood by philosophy unaided by revelation. 'Pure' nature is, moreover, unable to enjoy any form of relation with God, neither in its being nor in its knowledge. Its end, appetite and powers are all purely natural.[16] Supernaturalized nature is, in contrast, dependent for its existence on God, and explicable by revelation unaided by natural forms of knowledge. It is preserved solely by divine action and able to gain certain knowledge of revealed truth.

Aquinas and his later followers typically considered the question of the relation between God and humankind to be one about the way in which nature is ordered to its source. This approach is motivated by Aquinas's engagement with Avicenna and the Aristotelian philosophy promoted by him that was challenging Christian theology in the later twelfth century. Equally important to de Lubac is the Augustinian tradition, which tended to focus on the ordering not of nature but of the moral life. This was equally a product of a particular set of historical circumstances: Augustine's polemics against Pelagius over human freedom and action. The same fundamental question was, however, at issue in both traditions: the character of the relationship between God and humankind.[17] De Lubac is therefore able to identify an equivalent concept of pure *moral* nature in Augustinian theology.

Michael Baius (1513–89) argued that divine action on nature is necessary if human beings are to perfect themselves in accordance with their God-given end. He believed, furthermore, that this end is defined by natural means and not supernatural ones: not so much the vision of God as good moral conduct. The effects of divine action are, his doctrine implies, explicable wholly in terms of their natural effects.[18] In the Augustinian tradition that Baius seeks to promote, the power of sin over nature is omnipresent, and its effects are often discussed by comparing the nature of Adam before the Fall with that of Adam after the Fall, with Adam taken to represent the whole of the human race. Baius attributed Adam's good works in the prior state of innocence solely to the goodness of his nature. In other words, Adam had no need of grace until the Fall.[19] Baius believed that grace became effective in Adam only *after* the Fall as part of a new relationship between creator and creature.[20] This anthropology might appear to provide a positive affirmation of the intrinsic goodness and autonomy of human nature. Nevertheless, by denying that the human soul included within itself any spiritual quality before the Fall, Baius suggested that the soul is in essence a merely psychic entity.[21] This meant, in turn, that the action of grace on the soul after the Fall was in order to strengthen the soul to pursue purely *natural* ends. That notion had the effect of establishing, de Lubac argues, an excessively juridical conception of the relation between God and his creatures, with specific natural ends being granted or denied as rewards for particular good or bad acts.[22] Grace thus becomes omnipresent in a limited sense only, with its power fundamentally attenuated by being translated into purely natural effects.

Cornelius Jansenius (1585–1638), commonly regarded as the founder of the Jansenist movement which bears his name, conceives of the prelapsarian condition of Adam in a similar way to Baius's, although he 'has taken the theory to its logical conclusion, both in its fundamental principle and its consequences. His supralapsarian "optimism" has determined his practical pessimism.'[23] In other words, the more completely the goodness of his exalted, autonomous, natural state before the Fall is proclaimed, the more highly the intrinsic depravity of Adam's sin and its apocalyptic consequences after the Fall are magnified. Jansenius 'sees the grace of God now reigning over the ruins of a nature formerly master of itself',[24] and humanity as 'slaves of righteousness' in human terms[25] and absolutely. He believes that only a small number of people are elected to be saved, and that these are arbitrarily chosen. Jansenius also seeks to exclude all philosophical reasoning from theology.[26] Lastly, he maintains that grace entirely masters the will,[27] which becomes its tool. The significance of these positions will shortly become clearer as de Lubac's engagement with them is presented in greater detail.

BEYOND PURE NATURE AND NECESSARY GRACE

Purity of nature indicates, de Lubac believes, not goodness but separation and sinfulness. Why is this? The shortcoming of the philosophy of pure nature can be regarded from two standpoints: that of humanity, and – in so far as is possible – that of God. The first, human perspective is especially prominent in de Lubac's engagement with Cajetan and Suárez. This perspective supposes that human beings are naturally motivated to seek only natural ends, and that any spiritual end which they pursue must be given to them in an extrinsic (external) intervention by God which has no effect on their 'pure' nature. This natural understanding of the end which human beings seek fails, however, to acknowledge humanity's specifically spiritual character. Human beings are unique among all beings in the created order in combining material, intellectual and spiritual qualities,[28] but this had to be denied in often strident terms by upholders of the pure nature theory. Cajetan asserts: 'Nature gives the desire for the divine vision, and . . . cannot give what is requisite for such a vision, for instance the light of glory.'[29] Suárez contends: 'It is repugnant that an end be supernatural with respect to pursuit and natural with respect to appetite, since the natural appetite is found only in natural potency.'[30] An element common to these positions is that both deny any kind of continuity between grace and nature.

De Lubac argues that the work of Cajetan constitutes the key moment in the separation of nature from grace in catholic theology.[31] Although Cajetan claimed to be doing no more than commenting on Thomist theology, he in fact diverged from it on key points. This self-understanding contrasts with that of many theologians following him and Suárez, who stated openly that they were departing from Thomist theology rather than offering neutral interpretation.[32] In de Lubac's own time, however, the magisterium's reaffirmation of Aquinas's pre-eminent authority in catholic teaching had precipitated a revival of the Thomism of Cajetan and Suárez, but with this presented uncritically as if it were identical to Aquinas's own. De Lubac's fundamental objection to this neo-Thomism was that it presented nature as an order complete in itself to which revelation might be 'applied' or 'added'. Church teaching and tradition were consequently presented as originating in a supernatural realm and confronting a separate and already fully-constituted nature. This image of the relation of nature to the supernatural can be regarded eirenically as motivated by a well-intentioned attempt to safeguard fundamental elements of religion from false interpretation as merely cultural and social products, rather than eternal revealed truths. Nevertheless, by seeking to 'protect' the supernatural in this way, theologians made a major contribution to exiling it altogether from the modern world and allowing secularism to take root in its place.[33]

Aquinas's object was not to establish an ideal of the 'rational sufficiency' of nature, de Lubac argues, but to oppose it.[34] Neo-Thomism suffers, he continues, from an impoverished notion of finality very similar to that of the Aristotelian philosophy of Avicenna *against* which Aquinas was himself arguing, understanding finality to be a destination given to humanity from outside, rather than a destiny inscribed in its nature.[35] In naturalizing humanity, moreover, neo-Thomists effectively deny it the possibility of fulfilling its final end, which is at once both natural *and supernatural*. De Lubac pithily contests this stance, asserting: 'The authentic reign of the "supernatural" is never established on a depreciation of "nature".'[36] His attack on the theory of pure nature and its separation of nature from the supernatural is inspired by the work of the French catholic lay philosopher Maurice Blondel (1861–1949), whom de Lubac names as the provider of the primary impulse for his own efforts to recover a more authentic tradition of the supernatural.[37] Blondel had argued in his philosophy of action that concrete, practical activity is necessarily sustained by a power existing beyond the physical, concrete world in which action occurs. The supernatural, Blondel affirms

> is not an arbitrary 'something extra', a form extrinsic to humanity . . . It is an adoption, an assimilation, an incorporation, a consortium, a transformation which, through the bond of charity, insures both the union and the distinction of two incommensurables . . . [not] a sort of distinct being, a receptacle into which we are to be absorbed, emptying us of our human nature; it is on the contrary intended to be in us, *in nobis*, without ever being on that account something coming from us, *ex nobis*.[38]

The supernatural does not merely elevate nature or penetrate it, but transforms and transfigures nature.[39] This metamorphosis requires, as Teilhard de Chardin makes clear, *acceptance* by nature of the end presented to it: 'The supernatural fullness grows out of the natural universe according to a law of transformation . . . in that the supernatural actually rearranges the elements of this world to the point of making them truly more and other than what they were.'[40] This description of supernatural action suggests, like the Augustinian *in nobis ex nobis* motif of God acting 'in us, without us', a co-operative relation between grace and nature in humanity.

The second standpoint from which the philosophy of pure nature can be criticized is that of God. Prominent in de Lubac's critique of Reformation readings of Augustine is that they effectively compel God to offer grace to humanity. Baius states: 'Man was created to perform good works, just as the bird was manifestly made to fly . . . Just as the bird with broken wings cannot fly, so too man deprived of the Holy Spirit cannot act well.'[41] In other words, if humanity is to fulfil its God-given ends, both natural and supernatural, God is obliged to act to make this possible by redeeming humanity. Theologians who argue that it is human sinfulness which motivates God's redemptive action need to make their case, de Lubac argues, in a way that does not suggest that God is effectively compelled to intervene in the natural order.

A further implication of the supposition that grace is in this way necessary is that grace is offered in a specific, extrinsic act of divine giving, similar to the giving of a present to a child by its parents.[42] This conception of an exchange separates the gift of grace from the act of creation, however, apparently denying that the bestowal of life is itself an act of grace and perhaps the greatest act of grace. More seriously, this view of grace as given to humanity subsequent to its creation

> would not really or adequately express, in all its force, the radical gift of being which God has given me (inevitably we fall back into this language) by creating me. For it is a gift totally interior to me; nothing is left out of it, and nothing of myself is without it. It is incomparably more a gift than any outward, additional gifts which may later be given me by humans. There is no proportion between them; as an analogy they are infinitely inadequate.[43]

The foundations of a theology of grace are to be found, therefore, in the theology of creation, which is the real originating gift that God might *not* have given. God creates humanity as part of an entire universe that is at once both natural and supernatural, with the created order being continually offered a supernatural gift:

> God could have refused to give himself to his creatures, just as he could have, and has, given himself. The gratuitousness of the

supernatural order is true individually and totally. It is gratuitousness in itself. It is gratuitous as far as each one of us is concerned. It is gratuitous in regard to what we see as preceding it, whether in time or in logic. Further – and this is what some of the explanations I have contested seem to me not to make clear – its gratuitousness remains always complete. It remains gratuitous in every hypothesis. It is for ever new. It remains gratuitous at every stage of preparation for the gift, and at every stage of the giving of it. No 'disposition' in creatures can ever, in any way, bind the Creator.[44]

De Lubac emphasized this concept of the gift in *The Mystery of the Supernatural* in order to correct misinterpretations of his argument twenty years earlier in *Surnaturel*. It enabled him to focus on the twofold and thus paradoxical character of divine grace and initiative its continuity with human life is far from unproblematic.[45]

THE DESIRE OF NATURE FOR GOD

The idea that humanity possesses a natural desire for God has a long theological genesis.[46] This desire is expressed by many Greek theologians by means of the image of the incarnate logos gathering seeds planted by the creating logos. Justin Martyr distinguishes these two activities, in the course of contrasting members of the pre-Christian philosophical schools with followers of Christ: 'All the writers were able to see realities darkly through the sowing of the implanted word that was in them. For the seed and imitation imparted according to capacity is one thing, and quite another is the thing itself, of which there is the participation and imitation according to the grace which is from him.'[47] The redemption of the natural order effected by the life, death and resurrection of Christ activates, in other words, a potential for grace pre-existing in the soul as a result of its being part of divine creation. The image of God shines in the depths of this soul, which therefore is itself that image, and yearns to be reunited with the being on whom it is modelled.[48] The same essential notion is expressed in the Latin tradition, which uses the imagery of humankind being created bearing the (faint) image of God in order that it might share more fully in God's likeness. Tertullian, a principal proponent of this view of the soul, depicts the similarity of humanity to God as consisting in a shared capacity for reflective and productive reasoning, saying of God:

Whilst he was thus planning and arranging with his own reason, he was actually causing that to become Word . . . And that you may the more readily understand this, consider first of all, from your own self, who are made 'in the image and likeness of God', for what purpose it is that you also possess reason in yourself, who are a rational creature, as being not only made by a rational Artificer, but actually animated out of his substance. Observe, then, that when you are silently conversing with yourself, this very process is carried on within you by your reason . . . In a certain sense, the word is a second *person* within you.[49]

In both examples the desire of humanity for God is the result of divine action, whether by participation and imitation due to grace, or – what amounts to the same activity – through ongoing dialogue of the soul with God.

De Lubac also identifies the tradition of natural desire in the theology of Augustine. In so doing he wishes to challenge the simple postlapsarian view of God's adoption of humanity that was central to Jansenist theology and formed part of an effective denial that God's grace was initially freely given to creation and continues to be so given. According to the Jansenist view, which purported to be from Augustine, divine grace was given as God's necessary response to human sinfulness. In fact, writes de Lubac, Augustine identifies God's gracious activity at work at an earlier point in human history:

When he wants to establish that the divine adoption of man is an incomparable, unimaginable grace, he proves it not by alluding to our present sinful state, but on the basis of that universal reason – acceptable according to every hypothesis – that God has but one Son begotten of his substance, that by creation we have received human nature, and that adoption in the only-begotten Son makes us share in a marvellous fashion in the nature of God.[50]

God places humanity under grace, Augustine states, not by redemption but by adoption, and thus as part of the creative act. Creation is itself the original manifestation of divine grace and the manifestation which underlies all others. De Lubac adds, quoting from Augustine:

God has an only son whom he begat of his own substance . . . He did not, however, beget us of His own substance, for we are a creature which He did not beget, but made. And so in order to make us the brothers of Christ in his own manner, He adopted us. Accordingly, this manner by which God begat us to be his sons by his word *and his grace*, although we had already been not born of him but made and established, is called adoption.[51]

Denial of this adoptive grace specifically located in the creative act entails, therefore, either the supposition that humanity is composed of the same substance as Christ – which means that it does not require grace to be in right relation with God – or that human beings are not children of God and have no vocation to become so.

Augustine's theology of adoption leads him to argue that Adam lived under a kind of grace prior to the Fall. De Lubac summarizes his prelapsarian state as follows: 'The grace enjoyed by Adam was only a help without which perseverance would have been impossible, while now the justified receive the very help which causes them to persevere, the strength which wins perseverance.'[52] The implication is that Adam would necessarily have sinned if he had not been under a form of grace, and would therefore not have been responsible for his action. Christ's grace, in contrast, is a positive offering to humankind of the possibility of salvation.[53] De Lubac states:

> The grace of Christ as a matter of fact does not work in us in the same way as the grace of paradise worked (or would have worked) in Adam; it is more abundant, 'greater', 'more powerful', and we can be sure . . . that the divine goodness is more favourable to us today and the divine condescension more marvellous towards us than it ever was towards the man who had just come from the hands of the Creator.[54]

Part of the contrast between the grace of Adam and the grace of Christ derives from the different types of world in which the grace is effective. Adam was established in the midst of good, whereas humans are now born surrounded by evil.[55] Adam possessed merit by reason of his innocence and as a result of God's liberality, but current humanity is sought out by God at a lower starting point than Adam's. The simple fact that Adam sinned adds a further dimension. Adam fell because he possessed the necessary power not to sin, but lacked the will needed to actualize that power. The fact that successful perseverance is at last possible, however, means that grace now acts on human will not purely through God's creative liberality but as a consequence of God's redemptive mercy and forgiveness.

De Lubac's discussion of grace and nature also illuminates his consideration of nature and natural desire in Aquinas, which forms the crucial terminus of his argument. One of Aquinas's principal aims was to defend the possibility of the beatific vision in the face of the sceptical Aristotelian philosophy of his age. This motivated his argument that nature possesses its own integrity only by virtue of its dependence on divine action: in de Lubac's words, 'the *ordo gratiae* (order of grace) contains and perfects the *ordo naturae* (order of nature).'[56] God, in other words, is *naturarum auctor*, the originator of natures.[57] The sense of the containment of nature is just as important here as its perfection. Neither Aquinas nor de Lubac suggests that a simple passage from nature to grace can be achieved. To do so would be to deny the distinction which exists between the two, and to present nature as of virtually equal power and goodness to God. The importance and uniqueness of grace is that it provides the sole possibility of the perfection of nature in an operation wholly distinct from natural processes. Knowledge of nature is guaranteed by revelation, and not the reverse. Because Aquinas develops his philosophical apologetic as a theologian,[58] his distinctively Christian philosophy cannot be reduced to a set of axioms and related suppositions about nature which is then used to construct a system of doctrine. The point of Christian philosophy is, in fact, the reverse: that it subjects all natural and rational processes to the grace of God:

> It is not the supernatural which is explained by nature, at least as something postulated by it: it is, on the contrary, nature which is explained in the eyes of faith by the supernatural, as required for it . . . It is never nature which of itself has any call on the supernatural: it is the supernatural which, so to say, must summon up nature before nature can be in a position to receive it . . . In other and simpler words, the whole initiative is, and always will be, God's. In everything, God is the first. 'Before they call, says the Lord, I will answer them.'[59]

De Lubac points out that Aquinas explicitly refutes any understanding of debt based on the notion of just desert. The Angelic Doctor excludes the possibility that God can be indebted to nature on the grounds of nature's merits by arguing that grace does not necessarily need to be given as a reward for good acts. He also makes clear that, so far as supernatural gifts are concerned, nature cannot compel grace to act on it simply by virtue of its fallen state:

> Grace, inasmuch as it is gratuitously given, excludes the notion of debt. Now debt may be taken in two ways: first, as arising from merit; and this regards the person who performs meritorious works . . . The second debt regards the condition of nature. Thus we say it is due to a person to have reason, and whatever else belongs to human nature. Yet in neither way is debt taken to mean that God is under an obligation to His creature, but rather that the creature ought to be subject to God, that the divine ordination may be fulfilled in it, which is that a certain nature should have certain conditions or properties, and that by doing certain works it should attain to something further. And hence natural endowments are not a debt in the first sense but in the second. Hence they especially merit the name of grace.[60]

De Lubac demonstrates that natural desire as he understands it is not vulnerable to the same criticisms as pure nature and necessary grace – that it is an arbitrary construction of human reason. In so doing, he defends more than a simple natural desire (*desiderium naturale*) of humanity for union with God, which might well be optional and fleeting. By natural desire, de Lubac has in mind a desire of nature for God intrinsic to nature's very being (*naturae desideratum*).[61] He states of Aquinas:

> Without failing to acknowledge its nature, he could recognize in the human spirit something other than a totality closed in upon itself or upon this world; something other than a special kind of being seeking the way of perfection in accordance with its degree, its order, its natural dignity in the scheme of things; something other than a determined and determinate essence pursuing its stability, development and propagation: an impulse, a 'desire' by which man is led at least to understand that 'it is no longer a question of fulfilling nature, but of transcending it'.[62]

This explanation of the desire of nature specifically excludes the possibility that desire is simply natural or biological.[63] Created nature, de Lubac argues, is not a seed or embryo of divine being, and does not participate in any such entity. This means that natural desire cannot be understood as a capacity latent in the soul that is awaiting activation. The desire of the soul for God is, in contrast, a capacity for divine being born of a *lack* in the depths of the soul, rather than from the beginnings of a possession.[64] This is why Duns Scotus affirms that humanity is indisposed (*indispositus*) to its true end, which is not naturally accessible to humanity but gradually revealed to it. Only as a result of this revelation does humanity become progressively more disposed towards its end. Statements about the grace–nature relation need, therefore, to mediate two opposing principles: 'Return to me says the Lord of hosts, and I will return to you,' which overstates the initiative of nature in redemption, and 'Restore us to yourself, O Lord, that we may be restored,' which suggests that redemption is a result of a specific graced intervention.[65] Nature can in no way be proportionate to what infinitely surpasses it, although *is* raised up by infused grace.

De Lubac's opposition to the concept of pure nature, and to the notion of complete separation between nature and the supernatural, is motivated in part by pastoral concern about the disappearance of a sense of the sacred. This regard for the sacred provides additional and more concrete evidence that de Lubac is far from wishing to deny clear distinction between the two. After summarizing the doctrines of Aquinas and Augustine concerning the relation, he continues:

> There is thus an absolute distinction, a radical heterogeneity between nature and the supernatural, and it is good to stress this first in order to avoid certain deadly and sacrilegious confusions. But that does not prevent there from being an intimate relation between them, an ordination, a finality. Nature was made for the supernatural, and, without having any right over it, nature is not explained without it. As a result, the whole natural order, not only in humanity but in the destiny of humanity, is already penetrated by something supernatural that shapes and attracts it.[66]

De Lubac uses the term 'desire' to describe the response of nature to this supernatural action in it. The motif enables him to fuse an Augustinian concern with grace and moral liberty with the Thomist motif of the supernatural and natural liberty.[67] He concludes *The Mystery of the Supernatural* by citing the strident affirmation of humanity's election by Christ from Ephesians, in which these dual ideas of the transformation of material and moral nature resonate: 'Blessed be the God and Father of our Lord Jesus Christ, who . . . chose us in him . . . that we should be holy and blameless before him. He destined us in love to be his sons through Jesus Christ, according to the purpose of his will, to the praise of his glorious grace which he freely bestowed on us in the beloved.'[68]

THEOLOGY, HISTORY AND THE CHURCH

De Lubac, being an accomplished historical theologian, was alert to the tendency of creative and radical theologies to develop into systems of orthodoxy, frequently described as '-isms' and far removed from the intentions of their founder. To accept these transpositions is to commit exactly the error of which he had accused many Thomists in their treatment of Aquinas. De Lubac did not wish his own theology to be translated into another self-contained philosophy of pure nature. He states:

> I want to remain firmly within theology. I am not trying to establish a philosophical thesis, but to study a dogmatic statement and all that it implies. I do not say that the knowledge gained by reason of a natural desire, outside any context of faith, 'proves strictly that we are called to the beatific vision', and that therefore we can naturally attain 'the certainty that we have been created for that end'; on the contrary, I say that the knowledge that is revealed to us of that calling, which makes us certain of that end, leads us to recognize within ourselves the existence and nature of that desire.[69]

De Lubac's exhaustive study of the controversies surrounding the relation between nature and the supernatural had revealed to him the ease with which trenchant critiques of particular theological doctrines can mutate into the parody of the position they purport to be opposing. Critics of Baius, for instance, in attacking his belief that Adam, prior to the Fall, did not require grace in order to act well 'imagined that in this way they were waging a holy war in the name of Christian orthodoxy, thus preserving the salt of doctrine from losing its savour. Actually, without their realizing it, they were losing valuable ground, in some degree yielding to the prevalent naturalism and making the most dangerous of concessions to a world entirely unconcerned about its higher destiny.'[70] By contesting the excessive naturalism of the idea of pure nature with a theology in which all human goodness is due to the direct and arbitrary graced action of God, Baius's critics unwittingly promoted his project by laying foundations for a model of nature not necessarily dependent on God for its existence, but only for its salvation and redemption. The natural consequence of the view that some parts of nature were under grace while others were not was the development of a model of society as a secular entity founded in opposition to religious values and institutions.

De Lubac, by engaging the entire historical sweep of the grace–nature debate, prevents his theological agenda from being determined by his opponents. He also suggests that in so doing he is adopting a theological method closer to that of the Church than is the method of partisans of opposing philosophical positions. He observes that, so often, doctrinal 'expositions depend closely on the doctrinal battles that fired particular periods',[71] adding that this is especially true of discussions about grace. In the work of figures such as Baius, Jansenius, Cajetan and Suárez, he contends, 'polemical concern has outpaced the concern to build a complete and truly positive doctrine.' This is not to say, however, that their theological posturing has served no constructive doctrinal function in the Church. By being attentive to theological debates, de Lubac argues, the Church is not bound to accept their conclusions, but neither does it intend to pronounce on their value. The Church seeks, rather, to discern 'if such an assertion is or is not contained in her faith', and in the process of so doing 'interrogates her conscience'.[72]

The 'conscience of the Church' is thus challenged by theology, but also goes before theology, stimulating it, enlightening it, and leading theology to ratify its intuitions.[73] De Lubac indeed argues that the magisterium has in modern times supported neither the pure nature hypothesis nor a supernatural interventionism.[74] He contends, moreover, that the magisterium has tended to leave theological schools free to debate and to maintain positions contrary to one another and even to its own. One example he cites is Benedict XIV's admonition of the Grand Inquisitor of Spain for accepting accusations against certain Augustinians which had previously been rejected in Rome. Benedict, in his correspondence, 'constantly returned to the need for a multiplicity of schools within the Church'.[75]

Theologians are, de Lubac suggests, continually subject to the connected perils of granting both too much and too little to human nature and the various intellectual disciplines which describe it. He states:

> There is indeed an illusion of the absolute, but there is also an illusion of the relative; there is the illusion of the eternal, but there is also the illusion of the historical; there is the illusion of transcendence, and also the illusion of immanence; a mystical illusion and a positivist illusion. That is to say, if one misconceives the relative and the historical, one can, of course, only obtain a pseudo-absolute, a pseudo-eternal, and one's liberation is a dream. But, on the other hand, it is no less true that if we misconceive the eternal and the absolute, we are left with only a pseudo-historical, a pseudo-temporal, a path that does not lead to liberation. In short, 'mystification' takes place in more than one direction.[76]

If theologians allow social scientific disciplines like sociology and psychology comprehensively to define the human person and human needs and desires, they diminish both humanity and the Church's theological mission. Belief then becomes defined by the social sciences rather than being the faithful and reasoned response of humanity to God. No discipline which grounds its analysis and prescription in the natural or statistical sciences is able to describe the creative spontaneity and essential transcendence of human life caused by divine action in it and the implications of that action for human living.

CHAPTER 2

SPIRITUAL RESISTANCE TO NAZISM

Henri de Lubac's political writings and activities are among the most neglected elements of his theology. Two reasons may be identified for this. The first is that most of de Lubac's expositors have used his work to gain a better understanding of classic dogmatic categories like Church, Christology, Eucharist and Scripture. Political and social issues have simply not been the primary concerns of these readers. The second reason for the neglect of de Lubac's political theology is that a sizeable portion of it is contained in essays rather than full-length monographs. Some of these were anonymous, and others he did not collate until the final decade of his life.[1] It is now clear, however, that the context, motivation and implications of de Lubac's theology are profoundly political. Joseph Komonchak states accurately that, with his oeuvre, 'theology became an expression of the Church's engagement with society, culture and history and thereby regained the genuinely catholic, integral character it had lost during the time when it was considered to be mainly for domestic consumption.'[2]

PATRIOTISM AND THE NATION

De Lubac was, as a Jesuit, a member of a religious order which had been subject to sustained state persecution throughout his childhood and long period of formation. The most serious hostile acts occurred in 1901 and 1904. Known as the *lois d'exception*, these placed the religious orders at the centre of the conflict between Church and State which gripped France during the opening years of the twentieth century. The Waldeck–Rousseau measure, introduced on 1 July 1901, confirmed the right of free association for lay civic bodies, but required all religious congregations to register. Failure to do so could be punished by a fine or imprisonment, and provision was made for congregations not granted recognition to be dissolved and have their assets confiscated. The Combes measure of 7 July 1904 extended State discrimination against the Church by imposing a universal ban on teaching by clergy. Although targeted at school teachers, the legislation had the effect of preventing the formation of clergy and members of religious orders anywhere in the country. This is why the philosophate de Lubac attended was situated on Jersey rather than mainland France, and the theologate located at Ore Place, overlooking the town of Hastings on the south coast of England until 1926. In June that year, the Jesuit order decided to relocate the theologate to Fourvière, after twenty years in Hastings, following the appointment of the new Provincial, Jean-Baptiste Costa de Beauregard. De Lubac was therefore able to complete the remaining two of his four years of theological formation back in his own country.

It is a commonly-voiced opinion that the academic and religious vocations within the Church entail a retreat from politics and 'real life'. The story of de Lubac's own early life refutes this assertion comprehensively. De Lubac undertook his philosophical studies and half of his theological formation in exile precisely because he was a member of a religious order and studying within it. His consideration of patriotism therefore takes place against a highly ambiguous succession of recent historical events. De Lubac had, like so many Jesuits, served in the French armed forces during the First World War – members of religious orders receiving no exemption from the draft, not even in exile. This contribution of the religious orders and clergy to the war effort was, indeed, the main reason that the government granted tacit permission for the re-establishment of seminaries and scholasticates. Nevertheless, de Lubac's presence at Fourvière as a student was strictly illegal. He thus returned from exile to find himself 'living outside the law'.[3]

In his essay 'Patriotism and Nationalism', based on a lecture delivered during the spring of 1932, de Lubac distinguishes these two attitudes to the nation. He begins by affirming that a *patriotic* attitude to one's own people is a religious duty, adding that if members of civil society are sufficiently committed to its preservation, diverse forms of civic association will flourish within society in providential ways. The body politic is thus formed and preserved by the citizens themselves, and not by the action of government or other State authorities. Governments should not therefore attempt to limit participation in civil society by means of legal measures or coercion as this will rapidly erode the foundations on which their own power depends. *Nationalism*, in contrast with patriotism, develops from the regulation of civil society by the State in the name of national unity and purity. The principal error of nationalism lies, de Lubac argues, in the totalizing discourse which it assumes over every aspect of life, even religion: 'Nationalism is unregulated, because it considers the *patrie* to be *an absolute*, exalting it above everything, turning its interest into the supreme and universal norm . . . Such an attitude translates itself into language, where terms of religious vocabulary are appropriated one after the other in a process which begins with innocent analogy but ends in profanities.'[4] Establishing the *patrie* as the absolute political and civil entity permits it to assume a spiritual importance which can only rightly belong to religion. Furthermore, by appropriating religious language, whose ultimate reference is to a *transcendent* absolute, nationalist discourse impairs political criticism by suggesting that specific *concrete* events are inevitable and necessarily good. The effects of nationalist rhetoric are particularly explosive when one narrative clashes with another, because both claim to possess absolute concrete truth.

Christians are called to repudiate the politics of nationalism, de Lubac argues, but goes on to acknowledge nationalist sympathies prevalent within his own Church: 'There exists today – not only in France, but in France as elsewhere – in a more or less widespread State, a nationalist error, which it is important to guard against with all the more care because it tends to enter the consciences of Catholics more frequently than other errors.'[5] The right-wing Action Française movement led by Charles Maurras to which de Lubac here alludes was condemned by the Apostolic See in 1926, but its ideology continued to exert a forceful influence within the French Church until the Second World War. Maurras believed that human life is comprehensively determined by historical and biological laws, and considered liberal egalitarianism and democracy to be corrupt on the grounds that the human autonomy and freedom on which they are predicated are phantasms. Maurras was essentially an atheist who wished to preserve the utility of religion as a means of social control without accepting any of its metaphysical claims. His ideology was harmful in itself, but also prepared fertile political ground for the Nazi-controlled Vichy regime, which assumed power in France during the summer of 1940.[6]

De Lubac could not accept Maurras's conceptions of religion, humanity or society, believing that all three require a transcendent principle subsisting beyond the purely natural realm. Yet by subordinating Christian discourse to political ends, nationalist discourses such as that of Maurras deny the absolute character of this principle. This is especially evident in their concept of power, which replaces the classic understanding of temporal power as limited by an eternal principle with a purely pragmatic notion of a balance of power between competing political forces. The result in global politics is an 'armed peace' in which the 'world resembles a vast keg of powder which the slightest accident or blunder risks igniting'.[7] De Lubac identifies a long tradition of ecclesiastical opposition to this type of power balance, citing in his support the teaching of Leo XIII, Pius IX, Benedict XV and Pius XI.[8] In so doing he anticipates theological arguments which would be directed against Cold War proponents of nuclear proliferation, who sought to justify nuclear armament on the grounds that any nuclear war would be so catastrophic for humanity that its spectre was sufficient to preserve peace.

THE CHURCH IN POLITICS: POWER VERSUS CONSCIENCE

When de Lubac returned to France in the summer of 1926, the relation between Church and State was still being debated in terms of the rights which each enjoyed over the other. Two initiatives of Pope Pius XI (in office 1922–39) gave added impetus to these classic discussions. The 1924 encyclical *Maximam gravissimamque* had gone some way to accommodating the Church to the relation existing between Church and State in France following the 1905 Law of Separation between the two and the 1920 restoration of diplomatic relations with the Apostolic See by accepting the creation of diocesan associations comprising groups of local churches, providing they operated in conformity with canon law. The 1929 Lateran Treaty, enacted between the Apostolic See and Italy following protracted negotiation, clarified the political status of the papacy following the formation of the state of Italy in 1870 and the resurgence of Italian nationalism under Benito Mussolini by establishing the Vatican as an independent and neutral city state.

De Lubac identifies, in his 1932 essay 'The Authority of the Church in Temporal Matters', two types of power that the Church has, through history, claimed to exercise over the State: direct and indirect. The direct power doctrine is associated with Giles of Rome's treatise on ecclesiastical authority, which he believes is the source of all political legitimacy, and has its fullness in the papacy. Referring to the Pope, Giles states: 'The one who is personally spiritual and perfect is raised above all others by the purity of his conscience; the one who is perfect, spiritual and holy by his function possesses jurisdiction and power in abundance: he judges everything and dominates everything. The sovereign pontiff, man *spiritualissime*, cannot be judged by anyone. It is his responsibility to institute earthly power.'[9] Such a high conception of papal and ecclesial power as this had become, at best, the fiction of canon lawyers. It could be criticized, however, not simply on grounds of impracticality but because of theological flaws. The principal theological problem with this understanding of the Church's spiritual supremacy over the State was that it required the Church to exercise temporal power to which it was not entitled.

The alternative theory of *indirect* power was originally developed by Cardinal Robert Bellarmine (1542–1621). Pope Leo XIII (in office 1878–1903) had restated it in the encyclical *Immortale Dei* (1885), in response to this criticism and pressure of events. The indirect power theory suggested that the Church possessed jurisdiction over temporal matters 'accidentally' by virtue of its *spiritual* authority. De Lubac describes the subtle distinction on which this theory depended as follows: the Church could not possess temporal power, but could nonetheless exercise power in temporal affairs.[10] This teaching was motivated by commendable intentions, being conceived by both Bellarmine and Leo to serve as a 'dyke against the flood of absolutist doctrines on royal and state power'.[11]

De Lubac argues that, despite good intentions, the indirect power theory ultimately fails for the same reasons as that of direct power: temporal and spiritual power cannot, in practice, be separated. Theologians were disingenuous, he suggests, to have portrayed the subordination of State to Church as a purely incidental determination of temporal events by a solely spiritual power. He asserts, moreover, that 'making civil power a mere instrument of temporal power demeans the Church as well as humiliates the State.' When the Church becomes directly implicated in the vicissitudes of political life, it places its spiritual authority in grave danger.[12] De Lubac does not, however, propose the complete withdrawal of the Church from political matters. On the contrary, he affirms that the Church possesses eminent authority over everything in proportion to the spiritual element present in it. The Church's divine authority is nevertheless strictly limited to authority over individual human conscience.[13] The Church should not, for instance, seek to control or manipulate State apparatus, even in times of crisis: it acts on the State *only* by addressing itself to the consciences of the state's citizens. The Church does not exercise any power over the temporal order itself, whether direct or indirect, although its power nevertheless amounts to a 'power in temporal matters'.[14]

SACRED AGAINST SECULAR?

In a note prefixed to his essay 'The Authority of the Church in Temporal Matters' in 1984, de Lubac suggests that his discussion of the relation between Church and State, and between sacred and secular principles, is of merely historical interest. The essay addresses, he continues, questions that were debated during the early 1930s but have since been superseded. De Lubac could not have been more wrong in this assessment of his work's current relevance. In the brief period since his death in 1991, postmodern theory and political events have made decisive impacts on Christian theology as on other intellectual disciplines, and brought the question of the sacred–secular relation, and its practical consequences, back to the head of the theological agenda.

De Lubac's theory of the relation between Church and State can be understood accurately only in light of his theology of the relation between sacred and secular principles. This theology is illuminated by his study of Pierre-Joseph Proudhon (1809–65), and in particular de Lubac's acceptance of the French socialist's critique of Kantian and Hegelian dialectics. Kant had argued in the *Critique of Pure Reason* that four 'antinomies' may be identified within the human mind, associated with the finitude and infinitude of the world, the simplicity and complexity of the elements which compose it, the dependence yet absence of a free cause of being, and the necessity yet repugnance of a rational idea of God.[15] The essence of an antinomy is that it can be shown to be both true and false, which suggests that it is generated by human understanding functioning beyond its sphere of competence.[16] For instance, it can be argued on the basis of strict logic both that there must be an absolutely necessary being, because the chain of causes in the world must have an origin, and that there can be no absolutely necessary being, because its causality as part of a series of causes would be within time and therefore not absolute. Hegel, in his *Philosophy of History*, had revolutionized Kantian dialectics by conceiving antinomies as part of a larger movement of spirit (*Geist*) which formed human history and occurred according to a triadic rhythm of thesis, antithesis and synthesis of opposing ideas. The synthesis of the opposing ideas then provided a new thesis which would, in turn, be contradicted in a fresh dialectical movement of spirit.[17]

Proudhon reacted with scepticism to attempts to resolve the antinomies presented to humanity, believing against Kant that antinomies exist in being as well as in the understanding. He also denied, against Hegel, that antinomies can be abolished in a higher synthesis. The most that can be achieved between the two elements of an antinomy is, by contrast, *equilibrium*. Human thought and being are presented with a 'principle, in some way transcendent, which eludes dialectic and dominates all Becoming, and which is indispensable to them. A persistent antinomy – transforming itself into equilibrium – thanks to the action of a higher principle.'[18] De Lubac quotes with approval William Blake's poem 'The Marriage of Heaven and Hell': 'Without Contraries is no progression; Attraction and Repulsion, Reason and Energy, Love and Hatred, are necessary to Human existence.'[19]

It would be wrong to infer from this oppositional model of the relation of God and humanity that simple distinctions can in practice be drawn between 'religious' people and 'unbelievers'. This is illustrated at the level of personal faith in de Lubac's reading of Dostoevsky. Who among the great Russian author's characters is 'religious' and who is not? What about Alyosha, for instance, the youngest of the Brothers Karamazov? Does he simply provide a point of convergence for other more important figures, himself remaining spiritually insignificant because he has not experienced inner torment, committed murder or served time in a penal colony? Or does Alyosha's apparently naïve cheerfulness emerge from a spiritual peace and calm beyond good and evil: a place of profound self-knowledge and acceptance of the vicissitudes of worldly life and the turbulent Karamazov family? De Lubac leaves the question open – although in so doing presents a more sympathetic assessment of Alyosha than that delivered by many earlier commentators.[20]

The implications of de Lubac's oppositional doctrine of the sacred–secular relation for collective faith – in other words, the Church and its relation with the State – may now be considered. Historic discussion of the Church–State relation has generally identified ecclesial authority as sacred or spiritual, and political authority as secular. Biblical imagery has frequently been deployed to illustrate both the co-originality of this pair of realms and the different means by which power should be exercised within them. The two great lights of Genesis 1.16 have provided an allegory for temporal and spiritual authority, with the celestial imagery implying that *both* spiritual authority and political authority are of divine origin. Nevertheless, the two swords juxtaposed in successive chapters of Luke's Gospel suggest that the two types of authority should be exercised in different ways. Jesus's prophecy about the destruction of Jerusalem and its inhabitants describes the use of the *temporal* sword:

> There will be great distress on the earth and wrath against this people; they will fall by the edge of the sword and be taken away as captives among all nations; and Jerusalem will be trampled on by the Gentiles, until the times of the Gentiles are fulfilled.[21]

The sword is here wielded by the temporal power (the Roman Empire) in a way that is nonetheless providential, being interpreted by Jesus as part of God's saving plan for his people in which forces of sin and injustice are defeated.

This temporal use of the sword is in sharp contrast with the instruction of Jesus to his disciples in Gethsemane in the following chapter, referring to its *spiritual* use:

> When those who were around him saw what was coming, they asked, 'Lord, should we strike with the sword?' Then one of them struck the slave of the high priest and cut off his right ear. But Jesus said, 'No more of this!' And he touched his ear and healed him. Then Jesus said to the chief priests, the officers of the temple police, and the elders who had come for him, 'Have you come out with swords and clubs as if I were a bandit? When I was with you day after day in the temple, you did not lay hands upon me. But this is your hour, and the power of darkness!'[22]

The sword is here presented as an inappropriate instrument for a disciple of Jesus to employ. Jesus also suggests to his pursuers that use of the sword against the spiritual power he represents is sinful and the result of the working of an evil influence. For this reason, interpreters of the passage have inferred that the sword should be employed neither by the State to subdue the Church nor by the Church in defence of religion. In any case, it was clearly a convenient compromise for political rulers to be able to claim the temporal sword of divine authority for their actions, even violent ones, against political adversaries, and for the Church to be able to contend, also on the basis of divine authority but as represented in the spiritual sword, that it deserved exemption from any coercive treatment on the grounds that use of the temporal sword was delegated to the State by the Church.

This theory of Church–State relations rests, however, on the exclusive identification of the State as secular and the Church as spiritual. Such a clear distinction has found apparent support in the following key passage from Augustine of Hippo's *De civitate Dei*:

> Two cities, then, have been created by two loves: that is, the earthly by love of self extending even to contempt of God, and the heavenly by love of God extending even to contempt of self. The one, therefore, glories in itself, the other in the Lord; the one seeks glory from men, the other finds its highest glory in God, the Witness of our conscience. The one lifts up its head in its own glory; the other says to its God, 'Thou art my glory, and the lifter up of mine head.' . . . Thus in the Earthly City, its wise men, who live according to man, have pursued the goods of the body or of their own mind, or both . . . In the Heavenly City, however, man has no wisdom beyond the piety which rightly worships the true God, and which looks for its reward in the fellowship not only of holy men, but of angels also, 'that God may be all in all'.[23]

This statement was one of the founding texts for an entire school of Church–State relations grounded in the separation of sacred from secular and the supposed supremacy of the heavenly city (the Church), defined as purely sacred, over the earthly city (the State), defined as purely secular. The resulting tradition became known as 'political Augustinianism'. Among its principal defenders was Giles of Rome, whose argument for the necessary direct authority of the papacy over all other rulers has already been discussed.

The first problem with political Augustinianism, de Lubac argues, is that Augustine's theology does not actually support the doctrine. In fact, Augustine usually draws a radical distinction between the concept of the Church and that of the city of God. His two cities cannot, therefore, be identified with Church and State respectively, but are 'mystical societies, as secretly intermixed in history as they are adverse in principle'.[24] This helps to explain why Augustine was happy to retain Roman citizenship regardless of the religious complexion of the particular reigning emperor, which varied widely through the long span of his life. Political Augustinianism presents, moreover, a simplistic identification of the Church as sacred and the State as secular, the shortcomings of which are increasingly apparent. Modern political society has become adult, de Lubac reminds his readers,[25] and neither seeks nor requires theological justification of its legitimacy.

De Lubac counsels against understanding the relation between politics and religion in the modern world in these terms: 'Neither the spiritual combat which took place in heaven, nor the one that is still taking place on earth, in the daily life of human history, is to be seen as a struggle between two visible institutions, between two powers, one ecclesiastical and the other secular.'[26] De Lubac accepts that Augustine tended to absorb the natural order into the supernatural one, yet rejects the inference that this led him to assimilate the natural law of the State into the canon law of the Church.[27] Augustine presents two distinct *principles* of sacred and secular which are in practice mingled in the concrete institutions of Church and State. The true inheritor of his doctrine is not therefore Giles of Rome but Ignatius Loyola.[28] In his meditation on the two standards, Ignatius pictures Satan enthroned in the field of Babylon in a great chair of fire and smoke, summoning demons and scattering them throughout the world, in opposition to Christ, who is seated in a lowly place in the field of Jerusalem, choosing disciples and sending them out to all parts of the world. The two standards are not, crucially, identified by Ignatius with two different places or institutions, but with two different principles, one associated with knowledge of deceits and the aid to fight against them, and the other with the true life which Christ reveals and the grace needed to imitate Him.[29] Managing the tension and conflict between these two standards, rather than resolving either one into the other, is the true Christian vocation in political life.[30]

The real inheritors of Giles of Rome's direct power theory were his adversaries. Jean of Jandun (*c.*1280–1328) wrote his *Defensor pacis* in praise of King Philip IV of France and dedicated it to Ludwig of Bavaria, the Holy Roman Emperor.[31] Both these rulers successfully opposed papal power in machinations with lasting consequences. De Lubac remarks pointedly of Jean of Jardun: 'His religious theory is the complete reversal of the one Giles espoused. According to him, the *plenitudo potestatis*, which he praises unreservedly and conceives of as a physical force, belongs to secular power whose prerogatives have been usurped by the Church.'[32] Marsilius of Padua (*c.*1270–*c.*1342) developed a similarly extreme thesis of secularization, arguing that the secular government should assume the same functions as had been granted to the pope by apologists for theocracy. In other words, de Lubac suggests that proponents of secularization are usually responding to the usurpation of temporal power by the Church. The Church sows the seeds of secularization whenever it arrogates to itself the legitimate temporal power of political authorities.

CONSCIENCE AND REFLECTIVE ACTION

De Lubac shows how the result of the antithesis of sacred and secular principles is the emergence of conscience in human life. Conscience is the *unum*, the principle of all union and equilibrium in soul and world, and is as such transcendental. It is a secret bond between the human soul and the infinite, and therefore depends on the clear distinction between these two elements of the created order.[33] Conscience provides the basis for a dialectical relation between God and humanity, which is as such never resolved into a synthesis.

De Lubac prefers yet again, in his conception of conscience, an oppositional model of sacred and secular principles to one which emphasizes continuity. Indeed he even hesitates to use the concept of providence due to Proudhon's suggestion that its meaning is too close to that of the pagan concept of destiny or fate. The Christian religion is, in contrast to paganism, a 'revolt against destiny'.[34] Neither the Christian notion of providence nor the pagan one sufficiently defends the spiritual quality of Christian witness. This is evinced by the ease with which Nazism and communism were able to replace, in the minds of so many people, the belief in divine providence with the notion of fate.[35] Christians cannot respond by reversing this progression and reinstating providence in the place which fate has usurped. The new situation requires a revised theology of reflective, conscientious commitment to spiritual truth and its political consequences.

The conflict between God and humanity that Proudhon describes establishes a dichotomy between social spontaneity and reflective initiative, just like the neo-Thomist view of the absolute separation of pure nature from spiritual nature. Nature could, as a result of this separation, be considered to possess its own intelligence (whether termed destiny or providence) existing independently of the intelligence given to humanity to order it. This philosophy of nature would however be a dangerous one if it undermined humanity's sense of responsibility for the world. Proudhon's response to the problems which de Lubac identifies with the notion of providence would be that a *practical* or *methodological atheism* is needed to justify human intervention in earthly affairs. The legislator cannot assume that providence will guarantee his political ends because social improvement is dependent on humanity's exercise of its reflective will.[36] He recognizes that there may arrive a time in the life of a society when unreflective changes demand the intervention of free human reason in a new kind of providence which is *not* of this world. Christians need to act, likewise, *as if* God did not exist. God will not intervene to preserve the world when humanity omits to do so, but entrusts humanity with stewardship of his creation and with freedom and power to carry out this work. Freedom is the unique privilege of humankind which is therefore responsible for the universe: humanity, by the free decision of its conscience, completes the world, which cannot attain its end without human action.[37]

Conscience is the aspect of the human person which mediates between God and humanity by responding to the divine call. De Lubac makes a plea for grounding action in the purity of conscience rather than in complex rational justifications and compromises. A conscience which depends excessively on discursive reasoning has already departed from the instinctive spontaneity of truly conscientious action.[38] De Lubac describes the relational and responsive character of this human assent to God in patently Blondelian mode:

I can render this homage only if reflection enables me to discover in myself, beneath the appearance of servitude, a natural consent that mediates between pure necessity and freedom in the strict sense, an original assent springing from being itself, which the entire role of my free will is to ratify, whatever the cost . . . In a word, my entire moral life depends on the fact that the Being that gives me being is not a tyrant, that there is something in me that responds to his call, even more, that this call comes from that deep region which is more mine even than myself. In other words, everything depends on my being able to see, or at least to glimpse obscurely, the pure Love that lives behind the figure of the absolute Master.[39]

Spiritual witness of any kind depends on the growth of personal conscience within individual Christians, caused by the action of God and their own reflective consciousness, in which 'each one of us has constantly to be winning their own inner freedom'.[40] The human person is naturally oriented to assent, in their everyday living, to a universal, transcendent and absolute spiritual value.

SPIRITUAL RESISTANCE

The categories which had traditionally framed discussion of the exercise of ecclesial power over the State – direct power, indirect power, and power by means of influencing human conscience – were insufficient for the time of crisis in which de Lubac believed humanity to be living. He regarded the rise of the Nazi regime and the genocide perpetrated by it as a tragic and entirely new development in world history. Politics had always been an unscrupulous business, as testified by Machiavelli, but the systematic character of totalitarian violence and abuse of power was qualitatively different from Renaissance realpolitik. De Lubac states: 'What was at first a simple empirical recipe, a collection of maxims for the use of a prince without scruples, has gradually become a system, a totalitarian doctrine.'[41] Never before, he argues, had such heinous crimes been committed against a religious community by an avowedly irreligious regime. The spread of Nazism in France was abetted by the failure of the nation's political leaders to grasp this radically evil character of the regime with which they were contending. De Lubac protests: 'Pétain and his ministers, like most of the men of the Third Republic, seem to have been completely unaware of the formidable spiritual drama that was relentlessly pursuing its course and of the diabolical hurricane with whose violence any attempt to compromise could only intensify.'[42]

The rise of totalitarianism and the genocide intrinsic to it confronted de Lubac's political theology with a tremendous challenge. The questions facing individual Christians and the Church collectively no longer concerned the moral right of Christian intervention in the temporal realm, but the *responsibility* of Christians to defend basic human dignities and natural rights. At stake were not purely spiritual matters, but pressing temporal ones. De Lubac nevertheless believed the Nazi genocide to be part of a crisis in modern society of a fundamentally *spiritual* character. An adequate response to Nazism therefore required acceptance by the Church of its political responsibility to intervene in the events taking place, yet in a way that did not compromise but instead renewed its specifically spiritual witness in society.

Spiritual resistance did not prevent Christians from taking direct action against the occupying forces. The spiritual roots of direct political action needed to be preserved, however, and de Lubac considered this particular work to be his own personal calling. He had fought, shot and killed for his country at Verdun when conscripted into the First World War by the French State.[43] This was well before his ordination in 1927, however, and he regarded his priestly vocation in occupied France in different terms.[44] This is consonant with the teaching of Thomas Aquinas, who forbids priests from taking part in armed combat for two reasons. Warlike pursuits, being full of unrest, hinder the mind from the contemplation of divine things, the praise of God, and intercession for the people. They are, moreover, incompatible with the sacramental representation of Christ's passion on the altar. It is more fitting that clergy shed their own blood than that of others, Aquinas states, 'so as to imitate in deed what they portray in their ministry'.[45]

De Lubac's voice of protest against the collaboration of the Jesuit order and the French Catholic Church with the Vichy regime found few supporters within those institutions during the regime's early period. The terms of power and moral right in which Church–State relations had traditionally been framed did not seem to require the Church to speak out against political oppression, provided its own 'purely spiritual' interests were respected. Indeed the Vichy government, by finally rescinding the legislation which had technically outlawed the religious orders, had if anything improved the position of the Church vis-à-vis the State. De Lubac recalls his feeling of exasperation on seeing the large majority of French clergy employ 'naïvely supernatural' language to justify the collusion of the corrupt regime in the Nazi genocide. The occupation demanded a response from Christians precisely because it was the result of a *spiritual and religious* crisis, however. Political questions had become spiritual ones, and de Lubac was not prepared to compromise over them. In a letter to his superiors of 25 April 1941, he protested:

> The anti-Semitism of today was unknown to our fathers; besides its degrading effect on those who abandon themselves to it, it is anti-Christian. It is against the Bible, against the Gospel as well as the Old Testament, against the universalism of the church, against what is called the 'Roman International'; it is against all that Pius XI, following Saint Paul, claimed as ours the day he cried out: 'Spiritually we are Semites!' It is all the more important to be on our guard, for this anti-Semitism is already gaining ground among the Catholic elite, even in our religious houses. There we have a danger that is only all too real.[46]

Events began to unfold quickly. Persecution increased with the enactment on 3 June 1941 of a law requiring registration by all Jews. (This census would later enable the occupying German forces to identify, intern and deport them.) De Lubac and three colleagues convened immediately under the direction of Joseph Chaine to prepare the 'Draft of a Declaration of the Catholic Theology Faculty of Lyons'. The document affirms that Catholics possess the right to freedom of religion but only if they are prepared to protect that right for others. Its key paragraph immediately following reads:

> The Church cannot forget that the Israelites are the descendants of the people who were the object of the divine election of which she is the culmination, of those people from whom Christ, our Saviour, the Virgin Mary and the apostles sprang; that they have in common with us the books of the Old Testament, the inspired pages of which we read in our liturgy, the psalms from which we sing to praise God and express our hope for his Kingdom; that, according to the words of Pius XI, we, like they, are sons of Abraham, the father of believers, and that the blessing promised to his descendants is still upon them, to call them to recognize in Jesus the Christ who was promised to them.[47]

This document, known as the 'Chaine Declaration', had been conceived as a formal public statement of the Catholic Theological Faculty's position. De Lubac and its other authors did not attempt publication, however, before consulting Cardinal Gerlier, their chancellor, on his return from a visit to Spain. Gerlier judged, as had colleagues already consulted, that official publication would be unwise: no public media would be willing to undertake the task, and any attempt to solicit a publisher would rapidly attract the attention of the government, which would be likely to respond by closing the Faculty and possibly all Catholic Faculties in the city. Gerlier did, however, authorize clandestine circulation.[48]

This decision and de Lubac's acceptance of it marked a defining moment in his spiritual resistance. The anonymous authorship and clandestine circulation of the Chaine Declaration provided the model for the *Cahiers du témoignage chrétien*, the underground journal which de Lubac was instrumental in founding in November 1941 and subsequently editing. The *Cahiers* became the principal means of disseminating reliable printed information about the occupation and Nazi genocide elsewhere, of encouraging and exhorting the French people to spiritual resistance, and of providing accurate versions of papal pronouncements, which were heavily censored if they appeared in newspapers at all. The *Cahiers* also contained details of spiritual resistance to Nazism in other European countries, including excerpts from the writings of Karl Barth.

As the occupation progressed, de Lubac came under suspicion and worked with increasing care, fearing arrest or entrapment: collecting manuscripts from the houses of people who had fled; meeting with his colleague Pierre Chaillet, himself in hiding; editing and proof-reading each *Cahier*.[49] This work was undertaken, he confirms, with the tacit support of superiors, but they did not seek details of his activities for fear of compromising their secrecy. On one occasion, de Lubac narrowly escaped arrest by the Gestapo after receiving a warning via Charles Chamussy, the rector, from a contact in the prefecture that a round-up was imminent. Shortly after, Louis Richard, another of the Chaine Declaration's authors, was arrested and deported. Yet despite the increasingly determined efforts of the Gestapo to terminate the circulation of the *Cahiers*, their editorial and distribution networks were never decisively breached, despite one entire issue being seized and destroyed by the police. Their circulation continued beyond the liberation.

In view of recent renewed accusations made against Pope Pius XII (in office 1939–58), that he connived in the Jewish extermination, it should be noted that de Lubac regarded his own efforts to combat this maelstrom to be supported by and consonant with papal policy. Indeed, he understands the curial resistance as being, like his own, a fundamentally *spiritual* resistance, seeing Pius's mission as above all a spiritual mission which enters the temporal domain only to the extent that temporal questions are linked to spiritual ones. De Lubac spends considerable time discussing the so-called Bérard Report, prepared by Léon Bérard, French ambassador to the Apostolic See, at the request of Marshal Pétain, head of the Vichy government.[50] This document is theologically significant because it invoked arguments of Aquinas to justify the repression of Jews, presenting them as being the arguments of Pius himself. Measures which the report sought to justify in Thomist terms included the exclusion of Jews from exercising powers of government over Christians, and consequently from state administrative offices, as well as a quota system for the admission of Jews to universities and professions.[51] The text of Aquinas's which the report cited does not endorse any of these measures, however.[52] Indeed, in a case where 'unbelievers' already possess authority over believers established by human law, Aquinas states, this should not be revoked, because 'the Divine law which is the law of grace, does not do away with human law which is the law of natural reason.' Aquinas goes on to suggest that the Church is entitled to limit this authority in exceptional cases, but does not in practice often do so. The ending of requirements imposed by human law might for instance be justified in the case of a slave who becomes Christian receiving freedom from a Jewish master, but there is a danger of this causing scandal if applied on a larger scale. Citizens should, on the whole, honour the public servants to which they are appointed by human law, as Paul states, 'so that the name of God and the teaching may not be blasphemed'.[53]

The Bérard arguments were nonetheless publicized by Pétain and other members of the Vichy hierarchy in order to suggest that de Lubac and senior church figures who were protesting against the persecution were contradicting official policy. The arguments were later cited by Xavier Vallat, director of the High Commission for Jewish Questions, at his trial in defence of his actions.[54] De Lubac shows, however, that far from expressing the definitive view of the Apostolic See, the document, and especially its 'Thomist' section, was the creation of Bérard himself and 'not Roman: it was purely the product of an old tradition that was at once Gallican and clerical, exacerbated by nationalism of the kind that held sway at that time around Maurras.'[55]

During the war de Lubac resisted several advances from people who had become aware of his work and wished, for different reasons, to draw him from spiritual resistance into overtly political enterprises. On one occasion, a brother of General de Gaulle visited de Lubac to urge him to place his efforts at the service of the Free French movement, which de Gaulle was determined would organize and unify all resistance activity under his command. In another incident, an English agent arrived by parachute and also attempted, again without success, to solicit de Lubac's support. Involvement in these schemes would have compromised the specifically spiritual character of de Lubac's resistance to Nazism, leading him to associate with groups whose methods of operation and political motives were just as questionable as the Gestapo's. Other visitors tempted de Lubac to compromise himself by revealing confidential information, presumably with the intention of passing evidence to the authorities for his arrest and their personal reward.[56]

His work continued unbroken during the four years of the occupation despite these pressures and dangers. The most concrete policy which de Lubac disputed was *Service obligatoire du travail* (*STO*), which he wrote against in the first of the *Courriers du témoignage Chrétien*. (The *Courriers* were similar to the *Cahiers* in being clandestine publications, but were shorter, produced for a wider readership, and addressed more overtly political issues.) Under this work scheme, introduced on 16 February 1943, French students were required to travel to Germany in order to complete two years' service in support of the German war effort. De Lubac argued in his May article – which inspired the provocatively entitled *Cahier* of the following month, *Déportation* – that Christians should resist the sophistic arguments being put forward to persuade them to undertake war service for Germany, such as that they would be assisting collaboration between nations, and living in solidarity with the working class. The overriding requirement of justice, witnessed to by a pure conscience, calls the Christian to withhold support from any regime opposed to the Christian faith and determined to destroy the legitimate political order, and to assist others in withholding their own support.[57]

THE LOVE OF JUSTICE IN CHRIST

De Lubac argued that the vocation of France in the twentieth century remained a Christian one. The key to national renewal would be the recovery of this Christian vocation. The great Republican values of liberty, fraternity and equality are, he argues, inspired by the Christian religion and will atrophy if not renewed by it.[58] Rights are, moreover, sacred in a genuinely theological sense.[59] The Church, he asserts, 'was and always will be the source of human liberty and the mother of freedom' because it performs an essential and unique role in limiting state power.[60] In the State, there is always an 'obscure will to power, more or less conscious and more or less active – an irrational force of expansion that will not endure any obstacle and is impatient of all limitations'.[61] This is clearly a contentious view which would be greeted with hostility by numerous secularist republicans. De Lubac nonetheless insists that an inextricable bond exists between Christian witness and human dignity. This link is expressed comprehensively in the following key passage:

> The human person is conceived in the Church as having an absolute value, because they are created in the image of God, whose characteristics they reproduce by their spiritual properties of reason and freedom. Whence their eminent dignity; whence their call, their 'vocation' to a transcendent destiny, surpassing all the limitations of earthly ends. Inserted into time, the person breathes in eternity. 'God', says the Genesis account, 'made man in his image and likeness.' The Christian tradition comments: God made man in his image, that is, spirit like him, in view of leading him to his likeness, that is, to make him participate in his Life. There is, then, in all humanity a sacred part, which by right eludes any enterprise of slavery or monopolization: 'To Caesar what is Caesar's, but to God what is God's.' The depth of the human soul belongs only to God. Such is the final reason for that essential freedom that no one has the right ever to alienate and that assures us a being, a consistency, an inviolable interiority.[62]

De Lubac affirms that 'charity without justice inevitably turns into oppression and ruins the human character it ought to ennoble.'[63] Benevolence, good will or fine motives are not in themselves sufficient to sustain responsible political action. Respect for the Other rests in contrast on a principle which transcends the Other. De Lubac quotes the Stoic philosopher Marcus Aurelius in the course of his argument against the Jewish persecution: 'You have forgotten what sound relationship reunites every person with the human race: a relationship, not of blood and birth, but participation in the same intelligence. You have forgotten that the reasonable soul of each is a god, a derivation of the supreme being.'[64] De Lubac is especially concerned to defend the universality and equality of human dignity – a key Stoic idea and that tradition's principal bequest to Christian doctrine – against spurious understandings of the social implications of evolutionary theory. The evolutionary dynamics which govern animals, plants and other lower beings in the created order cannot be employed as political principles in human societies. De Lubac quotes with approval his friend and fellow Jesuit Pierre Teilhard de Chardin: 'I absolutely refuse to translate bluntly the mechanical laws of selection into the human field.'[65]

Humanity is defined essentially by its unique spiritual quality which sets it apart from the rest of material creation. This is reflected in both human conscience and mutual equality. The corollary of these two concepts is justice, which gives Christian love its content, and is like love founded on the mystery of God.[66] Justice reflects the divine, meaning that revelation amplifies the natural, human order of laws[67] rather than adding to them or invalidating them. De Lubac reminds his readers of words from the 1891 encyclical *Rerum novarum* of Pope Leo XIII, which repeat almost exactly those of Thomas Aquinas: 'A law deserves obedience only insofar as it is conformed to right reason, and thus to the eternal law of God.'[68] Justice subsists, Aquinas suggests, beyond the boundaries of individual conscience and even of humanity collectively, continually contradicting all unjust temporal actions.[69] De Lubac develops this argument further in his clandestine article 'Antisemitism and Christian conscience', in which he demonstrates how the Nazi denial of the full humanity of Jews is fundamentally a denial of the truth about the person of Christ, himself a Jew. De Lubac repeats Paul's proclamation to the Galatians that in Christ 'there is no longer Jew or Greek, there is no longer slave or free, there is no longer male and female; for all of you are one in Christ Jesus.'[70]

De Lubac pursues the argument that human rights and the right of Christians to unimpeded religious life are inalienably conjoined in a later *Cahier*, *The Rights of Man and of the Christian*, which he took a lead role in editing.[71] Because universal human equality and fellowship in Christ is the Church's core message, it is inevitable that the Church will be subject to attacks and persecution by anti-Semites. There is a necessary solidarity, de Lubac argues, between the Church and the Jews in times of persecution, with the two bodies called to exist in a relation of mutual suffering.[72] He contrasts this vision with the doctrines of the Nazi apologist Alfred Rosenberg, executed following the Nuremberg war crimes trials. Rosenberg presents Christ, in *The Myth of the Twentieth Century* – second only to Hitler's *Mein Kampf* in providing theoretical foundations for Nazism, as well as its most extensive theological defence – as the heroic leader of a triumphal movement, and a superman who has never conceived of the equality and fraternity of all of humanity in God.[73] Christian tradition has emphasized the humility, compassion and goodness of Christ, and the voluntary character of his sacrifice for the salvation of the world. De Lubac reminds his readers just how threatening this last Christian belief is to Nazi ideology, to which slavery and a theory justifying enslavement were intrinsic. In fact, persecuted Jews suffer with Christ and in Christ. Nazi ideology represents in the Jewish people in inflated form the evil and disorders of every human group, in exactly the same way as Christ has the sins of the whole world placed on his shoulders by his persecutors.

The Church, being the body of Christ, is called to an inclusive and diverse life and to present this life to the whole of society. The Church's beauty is 'resplendent in variety' and calls Christians to a life of solidarity with the suffering and persecuted. De Lubac holds in his mind the Revelation vision of the elect as a 'great multitude, that no one could count, from every nation, from all tribes and peoples and languages', and the baptism on the evening of Pentecost of 'Parthians, Medes, Elamites, Arabs, Libyans, Armenians'. In Christ, all former distinctions between Jew and Greek, free person and slave are abolished.[74]

CHAPTER 3

THE CHURCH

For the whole of his adult life excepting his war service, de Lubac was living and working in catholic institutions. His faith was formed by the Church and its sacraments, prayer, theology and mission. Perhaps with reference to his own experience, he defends the practice of infant baptism on the grounds that implicit faith provides its foundations.[1] The contrasting notion that faith is preserved, transmitted and confessed solely by explicit adult affirmation rests, he suggests, on a superficial understanding of its collective and historic context. In infant baptism, the child is received into the collective and objective sacramental faith of the Church. There then begins the gradual and unending process of making that faith an interior, lived reality, as the person who has been welcomed into the Church grows ever more deeply into a personal affirmation of faith and theological understanding of it. De Lubac thus lived intimately within the Church and also made sacrifices for it.

THEOLOGY AND CONTROVERSY

On 12 August 1950 the encyclical *Humani generis* was promulgated by Pope Pius XII 'concerning some false opinions threatening to undermine the foundations of catholic doctrine'. No living theologians were mentioned by name, though allusions were made to several figures by means of synopses of doctrines associated with them. One of these was de Lubac, hinted at in the reference to those who 'destroy the gratuity of the supernatural order' on the spurious grounds that God 'cannot create intellectual beings without ordering and calling them to the beatific vision'.[2]

The events surrounding the publication of *Humani generis* deeply affected de Lubac's life and theology through the whole of the 1950s. They can be traced to the Twenty-Ninth General Congregation of the Jesuits held in Rome during September and October 1946 to elect a new Superior General. On 17 September, two days after the selection of Jean-Baptiste Janssens, delegates were received by Pius XII at Castelgandolfo, the papal summer retreat house outside the city. In his address the Pope censured various theological tendencies associated with de Lubac and other theologians from Lyons: 'There has been much talk, but not enough reasoning in depth about a "new theology", perpetually evolving as everything else evolves, perpetually on the move but never getting anywhere. If we suppose we ought to indulge that sort of thinking, what will become of our never-changing catholic dogmas, and the unity and stability of our faith?'[3] This private address was printed the next day on the front page of the Vatican newspaper *L'Osservatore Romano*. The incoming Superior General privately assured de Lubac of his complete personal confidence.

Despite this affirmation, attacks on de Lubac by conservative theologians like Réginald Garrigou-Lagrange and Michel Labourdette increased in number and severity to the extent that Janssens – his hand forced by powerful conservative elements within the Society – informed him early in 1950 that in the summer he would be required to resign his editorship of the journal *Recherches de science religieuse*. In August he was relocated to Paris, and around November 1951 sent to an outpost of the order in Gap in the southern Alps. His books *Surnaturel*, *Corpus mysticum* and *De la connaissance de Dieu* were ordered to be withdrawn from catholic libraries and bookshops, and stringent vetting arrangements were established prior to the publication of any future works. De Lubac later described the absurdity of his position as follows: 'I was never questioned, I never had a single conversation about the root of the matter with any authority of the church in Rome or the Society. No one ever communicated to me any precise charge . . . No one ever asked me for anything that would resemble a "retraction", explanation or particular submission.'[4] De Lubac had become regarded as the leader of a radical theological movement associated with the Jesuit scholasticate of Fourvière in Lyons which had been labelled '*nouvelle théologie*'. It was supposed to emanate from the 'School of Fourvière', notably in a widely read hostile article by the Dominican scholar Réginald Garrigou-Lagrange, in language clearly echoed in the 1946 papal pronouncement.[5] As I have already shown, de Lubac had by this time already employed the term '*nouvelle théologie*' in an historical and negative sense.

Moreover, the theological tendencies identified as constituting *nouvelle théologie* were far more dispersed geographically and more intellectually diverse than critics were willing to accept. De Lubac himself resisted the notion that the collection of tendencies identified by critics constituted a school, as well as the assertion that he was their leading proponent.[6] In a memorandum prepared for his superiors in March 1947, he assured them:

> I do not have the temperament of a reformer, still less of an innovator. Far from ever having the idea of promoting a 'new theology', I admit that I did not even know of this expression except through the use made of it by the Holy Father in his address . . . I have neither plan nor purpose to propose. All the more reason for my not being the head of any school.[7]

De Lubac accepted without question the restrictions placed on his intellectual freedom. This was because he believed deeply in the spiritual value of obedience and suffering on the grounds that it brings about the concrete realization in consciousness of the fact that God is the final and absolute origin of all action and initiative.[8] Human projects, whether intellectual, practical, spiritual, or some combination of these, are always dependent for their success on divine power:

> All action that deserves to be called 'Christian' is necessarily deployed on a basis of passivity. The Spirit from whom it derives is a Spirit received from God. It is God himself, giving himself to us in the first place so that we may give ourselves to him; in so far as we welcome him into ourselves we are already not our own. This law is verified in the order of faith more than anywhere else. The truth that God pours into our minds is not just any truth, made to our humble human measure; the life he gives us to drink is not a natural life, which would find in us the wherewithal to maintain itself. This living truth and this true life find foothold in us only by dispossessing us of ourselves; if we are to live in them we must die to ourselves; and that dispossession and death are not

only the initial conditions of our salvation, they are a permanent aspect of our life as renewed in God. And this essential condition is brought out, par excellence, by the effect of Catholic obedience.[9]

In his reflection on the spiritual value of passivity and obedience, de Lubac was inspired by his friend and mentor Pierre Teilhard de Chardin, himself exiled from Paris to New York in the aftermath of *Humani generis*, dying there in 1955. In reflecting on Teilhard's principal theological text *The Divine Milieu*, he states:

> Passivities – as the very word indicates – are such only when they become ours: ours, by virtue of an initial acceptance or assumption, a ratification by the will; or at any rate from the moment when, reflected on by us and echoing in us, they cease to exercise their pressure simply as brute force, and present themselves to us as an actual interior state and as an attitude of obedience and love proposed to our freedom. They then become in a true sense *our* passivities, without ceasing to be other than us; and the operation that God effects in us through them cannot be replaced by any activity that we ourselves could initiate.[10]

Obedience is, therefore, a receptive disposition in which the subject becomes a channel for the graced action of God in the world. It is in this sense equally essential to both activity and passivity. Nonetheless, passivity is a more intense form of acceptance than one founded on the exercise of freedom.

De Lubac's quiet acceptance of his own situation might appear all the more remarkable in light of the fact that he was convicted of unorthodoxy and sentenced to silence not by a formally constituted legal process but by the misunderstanding and innuendo of people who were in most cases less scholarly and charitable than himself. This can, however, be the reality of life in the Church which commands obedience. De Lubac is profoundly realistic about the Church's character, which necessarily combines a 'mixture of the divine and the human within the visible alone'.[11] These imperfections are not aberrations of the Church, but proof of its need for redemption and inclusion within a greater spiritual unity. He is continually alert to the danger of drawing too sharp a division between the visible Church and the mystical body of Christ, such as is often produced, he avers, by 'undisciplined theological reflection'.

De Lubac states that the Church is 'something to be seen at the very heart of earthly reality, right at the core of all the confusion and all the mischances that are, inevitably, involved in its mission to humankind. My love is for the Holy City not only as it is ideally, but also as it appears in history, and particularly as it appears to us at present.'[12] He expresses the personal implications of this assessment in his statement that 'we have to consent personally and willingly to what would be a violation at the hands of any other power'.[13] Real obedience requires acceptance of suffering and injustice in a suspension of standard ethical norms.

Restrictions on de Lubac's intellectual freedom began to be lifted in 1956, when he was allowed to publish *Sur les chemins de Dieu*.[14] In the same year, he was granted permission to resume teaching Hinduism and Buddhism in the Catholic Faculties of Lyons. Two years later, four of his works were presented to Pope Pius XII. These were his two books on Buddhism, *Sur les chemins de Dieu* and *The Splendor of the Church*. In November 1959, de Lubac was allowed once more to teach catholic theology, before resigning on 1 March 1960. Five months later, his rehabilitation would be complete.

FAITH, ORDER AND TRADITION

De Lubac played a central role in the Second Vatican Council's deliberations. In August 1960, he was appointed by Pope John XXIII as a consultant to its Preparatory Theological Commission – a fact of which he first learned in a newspaper. He was later created a theological expert (*peritus*) to the Council, and then by Pope Paul VI a member of its Theological Commission and the two secretariats for non-Christian religions and non-believers.[15] These appointments provided extensive travel opportunities to address conferences in different parts of the world, including the United States, Canada, Argentina and Chile, as well as to develop friendships in Rome during frequent visits there.

De Lubac is characteristically reticent about the positions he advocated in the preliminary discussions, due not least to the oath of confidentiality he swore on appointment. The nature and scale of his contribution are therefore not easy to assess. Themes from several of his major works published prior to the preparations for the Council – *Corpus Mysticum* in 1944, *Catholicism* in 1947 and *The Splendor of the Church* in 1953 – are, however, identifiable in the constitutions *Lumen gentium* and *Gaudium et spes*. These include the mystery and ordering of the Church, and cultural development as dependent on spiritual and missionary impetus. At the very least, these works of de Lubac's articulated, disseminated and encouraged renewed understandings of the Church's mission and structures, particularly in relation to tradition and the Eucharist, in the conciliar and post-conciliar periods. These published writings, along with de Lubac's international lecturing, almost certainly made a greater impact on the Council than his participation in the preparations for it. The advance schemata were anyway all set aside by the bishops themselves at their first session during autumn 1962, as is well known.

A central concern of de Lubac's was to articulate a reinvigorated ecclesiology. This drew at a practical level on the concrete theological questions with which the Church had been confronted in France and elsewhere during the Second World War. The horror of the Holocaust had fundamentally challenged Christian attitudes to Judaism and its relation with the Church. The atrocities perpetrated had extended over such a vast area precisely because of the ease with which democratic and inclusive governance in historically Christian countries had been destroyed by ideology and violence. De Lubac was convinced that the Church had a duty to defend the values of liberal democratic governance against totalitarian incursions. This duty could not, however, be fulfilled by the clergy alone, but required mobilization of the entire Church. This is a key but neglected antecedent to subsequent developments in ecclesiology in which de Lubac's work was central, which sought to identify the Church with the whole body of the people of God rather than with its ordained ministers or consecrated buildings.

The Church, de Lubac affirms, possesses roots which far predate the birth of Jesus, having been prepared over centuries in the history of the Jewish people and prefigured in the earthly paradise of Eden. He states: 'Everywhere the Church appears in figure, in the whole fabric of the history of God's people.'[16] Images of the Church abound in Hebrew scripture: the tree of life in the midst of Paradise, from which flowed the four rivers of the Word of God; Noah's Ark in which the human race was preserved from destruction; the Holy Place where bread was offered and renewed; Mount Zion on which was founded the city where God dwelt; the tabernacle containing the divine commandments and the manna given to the people in the wilderness; Rahab's house in Jericho from where hung the rope enabling the escape of the spies of Israel from the hostile city; the temple of Solomon in which God was continually worshipped.[17] *The Shepherd of Hermas* is therefore right to depict the Church as an elderly woman, 'created first, before all things'.[18]

Such poetic imagery easily captures the imagination. The symbols it employs are nevertheless no more than types, or anticipations, of what was only realized fully in the mission of Jesus Christ. The Church

> begins in the wounded side of Christ on Calvary, goes through the tempering of the Pentecostal fires and comes onward like a burning flood to pass through each in his turn, so that fresh living water springs up in us and new flames are lit. By virtue of the divine power received from her founder, the Church is an institution that endures; but even more than an institution, she is a life that is passed on. She sets the seal of unity on all the children of God whom she gathers together.[19]

This identification of the Church's birth in Christ's Passion was fostered by the tradition of devotion to the Sacred Heart prevalent in the Society of Jesus, since the emblem of the bleeding Heart was given to the Society by its founder Ignatius Loyola. It suggests a mission focused on preaching and living the life, death and resurrection of Jesus Christ.

De Lubac traces the Church's institutional origins in the mission of Christ's earliest disciples, some of whom stood around the cross contemplating his death. This mission assumed, he argues, a concrete and ordered character from the outset. To adapt an insight from social philosophy, there is 'no realized community (*Gemeinschaft*) without a society (*Gesellschaft*) in which and through which it is realized'.[20] Finance, travel arrangements, accommodation, and the differentiation of roles, as well as their co-ordination, all feature prominently in the accounts of the nascent Church's activities in Acts and the New Testament letters. It is untrue, de Lubac makes clear, that the Church's origins are to be found in the small, sporadic, unorganized and often short-lived communities sometimes supposed to have formed the essence of early Christianity. A biblical model of the Church is therefore inevitably an ordered one:

> The Church as she is should be in verifiable continuity with the community of the first disciples, which was in turn, and from the

beginning, a clearly defined group, social in character, organized, and having its heads, its rites, and – soon – its legislation.[21]

In order to comprehend this continuity, it is necessary to look back before the Passion to the prior work of the apostles and disciples directed by Christ himself during his earthly ministry, and in particular to their calling by Christ. The Church is primarily a *convocatio*, that is, a body called by God in Christ. It is secondarily a *congregatio*, that is, a body gathered together in community.[22] These dual elements of its identity both suggest a need for order and structures.

A community context was intrinsic to Jesus's identity as the Jewish Messiah. Indeed, it seems unlikely that he would have been recognized as the Messiah had he not gathered around him a group of disciples formed by his teaching and who sought, under his direction, to disseminate it to others by deeds and proclamation. De Lubac cites with approval the description in Mark's Gospel of the group's formation by Jesus, who 'appointed twelve' to be with him for preaching and to cast out demons.[23] This number symbolized universality and the twelve tribes of Israel, and its importance explains why Judas needed to be replaced by Matthias following his betrayal of Jesus and subsequent death. Christian discipleship was thus from its origins a calling into membership of an ordered community, and its charisms were possessed and exercised as collective gifts.

The Church cannot be conceived in purely structural terms, however. The unceasing dynamic work of Christ within it always exceeds human interpretations and doctrines, and the Church is forever dependent on Christ for its justification and animation:

> the divine call that summons her into reality and the divine principle that animates her make her always anterior and superior to anything that can be enumerated and distinguished in her; you can say that she was born of the apostles, yet they themselves were first conceived by her. And it is this Church in her entirety who is, in her unicity and her unity, indissolubly a hierarchical society and a community of grace, under two different aspects respectively.[24]

De Lubac's ecclesiology is fundamentally motivated by his desire to make the Christian faith available in all its richness and power both within the Church and beyond the visible boundaries of the Church. This faith can, like any living reality, nevertheless only be transmitted in its various concrete and public forms, such as language, scripture, liturgy and teaching. The contrasting view, that faith will in some way be passed on to future generations without any tangible and intellectual content seems in comparison tantamount to superstition.

Faith cannot, however, be equated with the various individual forms in which it is expressed, because at its heart lie naturally incommunicable and synthetic elements. These are mediated to faith by tradition, which determines and sustains its forms of expression, rather than being exhaustively defined by them:

> Tradition, according to the Fathers of the Church, is in fact just the opposite of a burden of the past: it is a vital energy, a propulsive force as much as a protective force, acting within an entire community as at the heart of each of the faithful because it is none other than the very Word of God both perpetuating and renewing itself under the action of the Spirit of God; not a biblical letter in the individual hands of critics or thinkers, but the living Word entrusted to the Church and to those to whom the Church never ceases to give birth; not, moreover, a mere objective doctrine, but the whole mystery of Christ.[25]

Tradition is a 'principle of renewal' which ensures the 'perpetual youth' of the Church. It is the unfailing instinct that guides the Church and enables her to discern, with eyes fixed on Jesus, what best agrees with the spirit of the New Covenant. The Church's other elements, including theological reflection and administrative organization, are always subsequent to tradition, bringing to light and justifying, by reason and practice, some of the motivations underlying the practices which the 'vital energy' of tradition has passed on to it.[26]

De Lubac, despite his influence on the ecclesiology of the Second Vatican Council, believed that some of the Council's teachings had been distorted and wrongly applied. He described experiencing, during the Council itself, a sense of nervousness about the surrounding agitation for radical change.[27] He later protested: 'The Council is being betrayed, in its spirit as in its letter.'[28] He chastises theologians who believe that what is needed to reinvigorate the faith of the Church is the rewriting of theology and dogma, and who consider that they have achieved this 'chronological Manichaeism' of replacing a previous dark age with a future golden one.[29] He is even more scathing about the 'sheeplike spirit' of people who accept their pronouncements unquestioningly.[30]

THE MYSTICAL BODY

The Eucharist is the principal way by which the Church manifests and continues Christ's transforming action in the material world. De Lubac states: 'If the Church is real, she must be an organism that we can in some sense see and touch, just as we could have seen and touched the God-Man during his life on earth.'[31] Hence the Church's sacraments and the concrete elements they employ – bread and wine for the Eucharist, water for baptism, and oil for anointing – are of profound importance in faith and worship. De Lubac challenges a minimalist definition of a sacrament as being that which signifies only *something else*:

> Signs are not things to be stopped at, for they are, in themselves, valueless; by definition a sign is something translucent, which dissolves from before the face of what it manifests – like words, which would be nothing if they did not lead straight on to ideas. Under this aspect it is not something intermediate but something mediatory; it does not isolate, one from another, the two terms it is meant to link. It does not put a distance between them; on the contrary, it unites them by making present that which it evokes.[32]

The definition of a sacrament as sign is inadequate because that which is signified by a sign is separated from the sign itself, as illustrated by the fact that ordinary signs are provisional and more or less arbitrarily assigned to that which they signify. Road markings for instance vary from country to country. This is not to deny that the Eucharist *is* a sign, however. It is simultaneously a sign yet more than a sign because it performs a mediatory and unifying role which has no end. In the Eucharist we 'never come to the end of passing through this translucent medium, which we must, nevertheless, always pass through and that completely. It is always through it that we reach what it signifies; it can never be superseded, and its bounds cannot be broken.'[33]

De Lubac illustrates the everlasting quality of the Eucharist using examples from the liturgical history of Rome. Immediately before communion was received, a portion of bread consecrated at the previous Mass would be brought to the altar and placed in the chalice in a custom known as the *sancta*. Similarly, a piece of consecrated bread from that celebration would be reserved in order to be returned to the altar during the following one so that the mingling could be repeated. In another practice, the presiding bishop would despatch consecrated bread, known as the *fermentum*, from his own Mass to the priests presiding in the titular churches of the city, signifying the unity of the Church and its priesthood.[34] De Lubac also discusses a threefold understanding of the body of Christ which developed later once these ceremonies declined, when a piece of the host was simply broken off and placed in the chalice (the 'commingling') rather than being conveyed from the bishop or a tabernacle. In the interpretation of this practice, the portion placed in the chalice represents the resurrected body of Christ, the portion consumed by priest and people at the communion is identified with the body of Christ among the living, and the part left on the altar to be reserved is associated with the body of Christ which lies in the tomb.[35] The three parts of the host can also be taken as representing, respectively, the Church triumphant in heaven, the Church militant on earth, and the Church suffering in purgatory.[36] These various liturgical examples together suggest an understanding of the liturgy as continuous across both time and space, comprehending all believers past and present.

It is this objective and unceasing action of the Eucharist which creates the Church as a living organism, completing collectively the work begun in individual Christians at their baptism.[37] Although the Church produces the Eucharist, the Eucharist realizes the Church. It is therefore misleading to say that the Church realizes itself in the Eucharist. The correct order of dependence is summed up in the phrase of the writer to the Corinthians: 'Because there is one bread, we who are many are one body for we all partake of one bread.' Without the creative, life-giving power of this bread, the Church would be no more that a moral or political body.[38] The Church is, as many of the early Fathers insist however, a *mystical* body, in the sense that it originates beyond the natural order:

> By 'the mystical body' they mean neither an invisible body nor a ghostly image of a real one; they mean the *corpus in mysterio*, the body mystically signified and realized by the Eucharist – in other words, the unity of the Christian community that is made real by the 'holy mysteries' in an effective symbol.[39]

A possible objection to this position is that it suggests that the Church is brought into being only when gathered together and celebrating the Eucharist, and has no real existence at other times. De Lubac responds that the Church is in reality always united, simply by virtue of being a eucharistic body, but that this 'invisible unity must be visibly signified and visibly brought about'. The Eucharist is thus the primary instance of the concrete realization of unity, being a 'focal moment of intensity'.[40]

It would be easy to conclude that de Lubac's ecclesial definition of the Eucharist means that it is of primarily functional importance in establishing the Church as a community. He is, in fact, highly critical of such notions: not only do they regard the Eucharist as being little more than a sign, but in so doing also deny the Church's character as an organic body rather than an administrative entity. De Lubac states: 'We do not assimilate the nourishment from the eucharist; it assimilates us.'[41] He continues:

> The profound meaning of this doctrine and even its seriousness have often been neglected and sometimes misunderstood. Some people fear that it does not give enough weight to the dogma of the 'real presence'. But they are mistaken. How would the Church really be edified, how would all of her members be assembled into a truly single organism, which must be called ontological, by means of a sacrament that was only a symbol of the one whose body she must become and who alone can unify her? . . . Sacramental realism, ecclesial realism: the two are interdependent. Each one guarantees the other. Today, it is especially our faith in the 'real presence', clarified as a result of centuries of controversy and analysis, that leads us to faith in the ecclesial body.[42]

De Lubac therefore highlights a helpful distinction sometimes drawn in medieval conceptions of the Eucharist between three 'stages of depth, all three of them essential to its integrity': the outward signs of the sacrament alone (*sacramentum tantum*), which are the simple elements of bread and wine; that which is contained under the sign and signifies a deeper reality (*sacramentum et res*), which is the sacrament and the reality, the body of Christ; and the 'definitive fruit of the sacrament' (*res tantum*), being reality alone, which he identifies with the unity of the Church.[43] A full appraisal of the Christological significance of each of these three aspects situates eucharistic reality both in the material reality provided by the elements of bread and wine *and* in the church community which they nourish.

De Lubac develops his historical theology of the Eucharist preeminently in *Corpus Mysticum*. His central thesis here concerns the understanding of the different dimensions of the body of Christ and their mutual relation:

> Of the three terms: historical body, sacramental body and ecclesial body, that were in use . . . the caesura was originally placed between the first and the second, whereas it subsequently came to be placed between the second and the third. Such, in brief, is the fact that dominates the whole evolution of eucharistic theories.[44]

The study is at one level descriptive, yet de Lubac is passionately concerned in the course of his narrative to challenge the diminished theology of the Church that this historical evolution suggests. He points out that around the ninth century the host was described as the 'mystical' body of Christ in order to *distinguish* it from the historical body born of Mary, rather than – as would later happen – to buttress sometimes 'overly individualistic devotion' and 'sentimental excesses'.[45] Yet he is at equal pains to demonstrate how a view of the ecclesial body as sacramental need not be at the expense of the belief that in the Eucharist we receive sacramentally the historical body of Christ.

Our reception of the host is frequently presented as consumption, but de Lubac offers a reverse perspective: that in the words of Augustine, 'You will not change me into you, as you do with the food of your body. Instead you will be changed into me.'[46] Indeed the Eucharist as mystery is essentially active, 'worked, celebrated, offered, completed, interrupted, restarted, frequented', and only as a result of this activity is the Eucharist as sacrament able to be 'carried, deposed, kept, divided, broken, distributed, received, absorbed, eaten and drunk'.[47] This active dimension of Eucharist points us to its future-oriented aspect: *anticipation* is just as important a part of eucharistic theology as memorial and presence, and constitutes moreover their fullest expression. It enables, furthermore, a partial redemption of the sign: the Eucharist is an effective sign precisely because it is a sacrament, bringing into the present a new reality that did not previously exist:

The eucharist is not simply oriented towards the past, dependent on Calvary. It is also oriented towards a future, which in turn depends on it: the building up of the Church and the coming of the 'truth'. Thus it has a double symbolism. It is a sacrament of memory but also a sacrament of hope. *A pledge and image of the reality to come.* It does not only reproduce, it also anticipates: *pre-signs, pre-figures, pre-demonstrates.* In its own turn it also makes present and makes present by signifying. It is the effective sign, most particularly, of the *body of Christ which is the Church*; it is the effective sign of the fraternal charity which binds its members . . . it is the effective sign of the peace and unity for which Christ died and towards which we are reaching, moved by his Spirit. . . It therefore signifies us to ourselves – *our own mystery, a figure of our-selves* – in what we have already begun to be through baptism (*one baptism*), but above all in what we ought to become: in this sacrament of unity, *is prefigured what we will become in the future.*[48]

This anticipatory view of the Eucharist is expressed in the fraction (breaking) of the host which represents the Church, which although existing in many parts is nevertheless one.[49]

In light of these reflections, what is the status of the eucharistic substance itself? The Eucharist is frequently defined in terms of the 'transubstantiation' of the species, with the 'substance' consisting of the 'true' body and blood of Christ whilst the 'accidents' of the bread and the wine remain unchanged. The sacrament is, under this view, a 'container' or 'envelope' of the mystery hidden within it.[50] Concepts such as these encourage, however, exclusive focus on the transformation of the species at the expense of the transformation of the Church. De Lubac points out how the older term 'confection' has been used to describe the change undergone in both bread and wine, *and* believer and Church as the believer is brought into the Church.[51] This sense of synthetic transformation is evident in medieval mystics like Catherine of Siena and even in John Calvin.[52] Yet the impending Counter Reformation tended to identify the host as the *true* body 'moulded into one' with the historical body of Christ,[53] and the Church as the *mystical* body no longer in relation with the Eucharist but in contrast to the secular State. 'Mystical body' thus became a synonym for 'mystical flesh', against which Protestant reformers defined their own notion of the 'spiritual body' of the Eucharist separable from concrete mystical notions of the body of Christ present as substance.[54] In consequence, theories of the Church began to develop outside any sacramental framework in both Catholic and Reformed traditions.

Bound up with this notion of a 'true' body is a whole theological system in which the 'viewpoint of action . . . yields before the view-point of presence, and the consideration of different states equally gives way to that of essence or of identical substance'.[55] De Lubac complains: 'Eucharistic theology became more and more a form of apologetic and organized itself increasingly round a defence of the "real presence". Apology for dogma succeeded the understanding of faith.'[56] The terms in which this fixation on the truth of presence were articulated are shown in the striking but theologically dubious words in which Berengar of Tours was forced to recant: 'It is sensu-ally that (the body of Christ) is handled and broken by the priests and chewed by the faithful.'[57]

A point of terminology bedevilled these discussions: 'the tempta-tion of . . . considering "mystical" as a watering-down of "real" or of "true".'[58] On the contrary, de Lubac argues, the language of the host as mystical body revealed the full extent of its transforming action on the Church:

> Eucharistic realism and ecclesial realism: these two realisms support one another, each is the guarantee of the other. Ecclesial realism safeguards eucharistic realism and the latter confirms the former. The same unity of the Word is reflected in both. Today, it is above all our faith in the 'real presence', made explicit thanks to centuries of controversy and analysis, that introduces us to faith in the ecclesial body: effectively signified by the mystery of the altar, the mystery of the Church has to share the same nature and the same depth. Among the ancients, the perspective was often inverted. The accent was habitually placed on the effect rather than on the cause. But the ecclesial realism to which they universally offer us the most explicit testimony is at the same time, and when necessary, the guarantee of their eucharistic realism.[59]

This insight into the possibility of different routes to deeper appre-ciation of the Eucharist also holds true at a personal level: depend-ing on many circumstances, some people might be drawn into church membership after being seized by a sense of the holiness of worship, whereas others might grow into this later following practical involvement in church guilds or community groups associated with the Church.

De Lubac offers a yet larger perspective on the Eucharist based on the notion of the whole of creation being continually transformed in analogical representation of the worship of heaven. He states of the Eucharist:

> It is not specifically liturgical. Far from restricting itself to describing a ceremony, or a figurative or commemorative act, it reaches out to cover the whole order of the Incarnation – unless we prefer to say . . . that this whole order of the redemptive Incarnation should itself be considered as a vast liturgy, the earthly and temporal image of the eternal liturgy which is taking place in heaven.[60]

De Lubac is inspired here by Teilhard de Chardin's notion of the 'extensions' of the Eucharist. The physical transformation of the host is not, Teilhard argues, confined within the visible surface of the bread, and not even within the membership of the visible universal Church. Rather the 'priestly function extends to the growth of the mystical body and the consecration of the cosmos'.[61] De Lubac quotes Teilhard: 'When the priest says the words *Hoc est Corpus meum*, his words fall directly on to the bread and directly transform it into the individual reality of Christ. But the great sacramental operation does not cease at that local and momentary event.'[62] Teilhard believes that the transformative action of Christ cannot be restricted to the matter of the particular eucharistic host, and communicates this intuition in one place with the image of the whole of creation as an altar: nature is matter offered to the supernatural.[63]

Such imagery might seem overblown. Yet it is a constructive attempt to apply some of the classic dogmatic categories like consecration, as they have evolved through the history of eucharistic theology, to the theological and pastoral question of the meaning of Eucharist and creation. 'Preserving the status quo in theories and viewpoints has never been and can never be,' de Lubac states, 'an adequate means of safeguarding the truth.'[64] Teilhard, he affirms, 'in no way regards the world as sacred in itself', although does see it as 'wholly "sacralized" by the universal presence of its Creator'. Moreover 'he sees it as "consecrated" by the presence of the risen

Christ, his "immortal and unifying" presence radiating through the eucharist . . . Such a concept of the "consecration of the world" is therefore equally far removed from the secularist theory and from that which attributes to the world, in itself and by itself, a sacred character.'[65] This provides another perspective on the theology of the *surnaturel*: that the whole of creation is offered, uplifted and transformed by human action and divine response. The Eucharist reveals to humanity the fundamentally concrete and material character of this liturgy.

PARTICULAR AND LOCAL CHURCHES IN THE UNIVERSAL CHURCH

The Church's continual birth out of a dynamic unity preserved by the Eucharist provides the proper basis for consideration of its institutional structure. Key in this discussion is the relation of the *particular* church to the *universal* Church: how, in other words, does the Church become incarnated in specific places and localities while retaining its unity and distinctive attributes? Its identity originates in a direct continuity with the people of Israel.[66] The Hebrew concept of 'Qahal' (assembly), translated 'ecclesia' in the Septuagint, does not refer to a 'restricted group or a purely empirical gathering, but the whole people of God, a concrete reality which, however small it may seem outwardly, is yet always far greater than it appears'. In the Jewish context, the 'national character of the kingdom of God, in apparent contradiction with its worldwide character, was an antidote to all attempts at interpretation in an individualist sense'.[67] It is only through this concrete fusion in Israel of particularity and universality that God reveals and furthers his purpose to humankind as a whole.

These Jewish antecedents contribute to a model for understanding the universal Church, which consists, de Lubac argues, of various particular churches. Each particular church is presided over by a bishop[68] who ensures its universal and centripetal identity, as exemplified in the liturgical practice previously described of despatching the *fermentum* to the surrounding churches during the Eucharist. The character of particular churches is primarily theological: they are 'particular' in the sense that they comprise specific instances of the Church, which is universal. All particular churches 'proceed from a prior, concrete church, that of Jerusalem', and not from divisions of a previously undifferentiated universal Church,[69] nor even from a standard model based on the church in Rome.

De Lubac distinguishes the concept of the particular church from that of the *local* church. While a particular church is such only because it is fully universal, a local church possesses as an essential part of its character features which distinguish it from the universal Church. Local churches 'have something contingent in their very structure, and the factors which have contributed to their formation are, at least in part, of the merely human order'.[70] Criteria for their formation are largely socio-cultural. This is not to deny the importance or validity of local churches as ecclesial communities. They are, indeed, useful and even indispensable to the universal Church[71] in rooting its life in specific cultural forms:

> A rich element of human variety is joined with the element of divine unity brought by the first founders, all moved by the one Spirit, as a message through which the personality of each of them is already reflected. Thus is brought about that union of the supernatural and 'nature' (which is to say, here, of the human, of culture), by which all that is authentically catholic is recognized.[72]

A local church is not necessarily a small one, and can in principle cover an entire continent. Its defining characteristic is rather that it is always formed from the combined mission of one or more particular churches.[73] De Lubac cites the examples of the Consejo Episcopal Latinoamericano (CELAM), the group of all Latin American churches, as a 'very vast' local church, and the annual Fulda conference of German bishops.[74] The undoubtedly large contributions of local churches to the mission of the universal Church serves as a reminder that the Church is not a uniformity but a pluriformity. De Lubac employs Ignatius of Antioch's image of the Church being 'like a great lyre'. Its beauty is, he affirms, resplendent in variety.[75]

This pluriformity is, however, entirely different from a 'unilateral and immoderate exaltation of doctrinal pluralism'.[76] It is precisely on a common doctrine of what constitutes the Church that its universality, and hence its particularity, are derived. Diversity of witness is to be promoted because it grounds the Church's identity and mission ever more deeply in specific cultures. Nevertheless, doctrinal pluralism touching basic elements of that identity and mission should be resisted because it undermines them. Consider for instance national churches, such as the 'Church of England'. Such terms possess a 'practical value of designation'. If taken as referring to a separated church founded on a distinct doctrinal basis, however, they then suggest a 'diminished understanding of the mystical reality of both the particular church and the universal Church'.[77] In this case, cultural identity has undermined the Church's realization of its universal identity rather than intensified it. De Lubac perceptively identifies how religious divisions and schisms have normally occurred along cultural boundaries as a result of sociological pressures.[78] There exists, in this way, a direct tension between nationalism and catholicity generated by the tendency to exclusivism inherent in all secular culture. Nationalism is, however, an aberration of true culture, which possesses an 'open and universalizing character'.[79] It is the mission of the Church to subvert all exclusivist cultural discourses and thereby demonstrate the transcendent and spiritual character of all genuine culture.

Considerable scope clearly remains for different interpretations of what precisely are the essential unalterable marks of the universal Church and its particular churches. Nevertheless, the distinction between universality, particularity and locality provides a useful framework for thinking about the concrete ways in which churches are called to preserve and promote their unity in diversity. Christians from a wide variety of local traditions should be able to agree that their identity and mission need to possess some kind of universal dimension, especially in a world that is itself increasingly global. Indeed, the validity of mission could even be said to rest on the extent to which it aims to incorporate people into the universal Church. On this point de Lubac quotes an emphatic statement of Michael Ramsey, a former Archbishop of Canterbury: 'A local church can claim the loyalty of the Christian with respect to herself only by leading him beyond herself to the universal family she represents. The catholic structure is therefore not a hierarchical tyranny but a means of deliverance through an incorporation into the Gospel of God, of the Church of all times.'[80]

De Lubac discusses and defends at length the role of the church in Rome in maintaining and fostering the Church's universal identity. Its calling to act as the focal point of ecclesial unity is grounded, significantly, in its own identity as a particular church.[81] A corollary is that the Roman church is, when exercising its universal ministry, itself bound by the requirements of universality which pertain to any particular church. An early instance of its universal ministry in action is the letter despatched by Clement of Rome to the church in Corinth.[82] This letter originated from Clement even though the apostle John was still alive and Ephesus was situated closer to Corinth than was Rome. This is because Rome was at the centre, de Lubac argues, of a comprehensive network of particular churches, preserved by means of letters of communion, in which its bishop had acquired the role of arbiter.[83] The universal Roman primacy rests, in other words, neither on a claim that it is the most ancient particular church – in fact, the church in Jerusalem predated it – nor on a lineage of missions and church foundations emanating from Rome. The Petrine succession was, instead, first affirmed 'peacefully by simple practice, and not by theoretical expositions, claims and an arsenal of proofs'.[84] A theoretical origin should, de Lubac adds, arouse reasonable suspicion, suggesting an exercise whose aim was to coerce recalcitrant churches into accepting an imposed novelty. The relation between tradition and theology is, in this case as in others, the reverse: theological justifications 'do not come of necessity to transform a fact into a right' but to 'show the right of the fact'.[85]

This analysis of the basis of the Roman primacy poses several points for further reflection. The Roman claim cannot be dismissed with many of the standard objections which de Lubac shows are in fact irrelevant to it. Nevertheless, the picture which emerges is one of a ministry exercised pragmatically through encouragement, advice, cajoling or reprimand, rather than by means of legal apparatus.

A further pertinent point concerns the implications of the origin of Rome's universal ministry in its own particularity for an understanding of that ministry. De Lubac regards as inessential the internationalization of the church in Rome, whether in staff appointments or the method of papal elections. The role of the cardinals originates in the practice of bishops of neighbouring dioceses gathering together on news of the death of a bishop for the election and ordination of his successor. The cardinal bishops are therefore the bishops of the suburbicarian Roman dioceses.[86] The main advantage of this practice is pragmatic, ensuring that the chosen successor is likely to receive approval from the whole Church. De Lubac accepts that some decentralization of church decision-making, known as 'subsidiarity', can be useful.[87] There nevertheless remains the danger of replicating a single administrative and bureaucratic processes within each diocese. Moreover, subsidiarity means accepting with full seriousness the responsibility for making decisions: it cannot be construed simply as providing an entitlement to make different decisions. He portrays the focal role of the modern church in Rome in pragmatic terms strikingly similar to those used in the discussion of Clement's epistle to the Corinthians:

> It is naturally at Rome, the centre of catholicity, that the vast work of research and clarification called forth by the last council in matters of liturgy, canon law, theology, and pastoral practice for the purpose of the desired renewal comes together today. It is at Rome that the experts coming from the four corners of the world to achieve this end most often meet. It is therefore at Rome that the more or less provisional fruit of all this work flows back.[88]

THE BISHOP

Bishops combine universality and particularity in their ministry to particular churches, as has already been discussed. They thus become fathers for the Church which first gave birth to them.[89] If the bishops are the servants (*ministri*) of the Christian people, it is because they are, first of all, the servants of God and of Jesus Christ among the people.[90] Their service is exercised with authority on behalf of God and therefore legitimately demands obedience. De Lubac, as has previously been seen, was himself entirely content to submit to the Church's authority, which he describes as 'perhaps the most secret point in the mystery of faith' and therefore the 'hardest to access by a mind that has not been converted by the Spirit of God'.[91]

One aspect of the universality of episcopal authority is that it is not fundamentally limited to the diocese in which the bishop has particular pastoral authority. If this were the case, then the status of the Petrine ministry itself, rooted in the particular church of Rome, would be called into question. An example of this wider exercise of episcopal responsibility is Augustine's attack on the errors of Pelagius, which were of little concern to the people of his backwater diocese.[92] The question of when it is appropriate for one bishop to intervene in the affairs of another diocese will, of course, depend on a complex interaction of theological and administrative considerations and occur in close co-operation with the bishops whose function it is to preserve the Church's overall unity.

The authority of the bishop is collegial and universal, but bishops do not need to be assembled in a single place in order to exercise it. The exchange of spiritual letters, dating back to Clement's *First Epistle*, provides one example of how episcopal ministry may be exercised collegially today in a Church that is widely dispersed geographically.[93] De Lubac states: 'It is not only through decisions made in council, but more usually through the unanimous teaching of its members, dispersed in space and spread out in time, that the episcopal college watches over and orders the faith and life of the Christian community.'[94] Every episcopal action is collegial, although not usually an act of bishops gathered in one place. De Lubac states: 'We can never remind ourselves too frequently of the essentially universal nature of the collegial bond and the solicitude which each bishop must have personally, in virtue of this bond, for the universal Church.'[95]

He reserves the adjectives 'collective' and 'conjoint' to describe the actions of the bishops gathered together in one place, most recently at the Second Vatican Council.[96] The dichotomy between collective or conjoint action, and collegial action, leaves intermediary institutions and gatherings with no theologically specified function. The permanent offices of episcopal conferences are not, for instance, organs of collegiality,[97] having added nothing to the essentially collegial nature of the authority of individual bishops in their dioceses and the wider Church. De Lubac vehemently opposes, for similar reasons, the 'phantasm of conciliarism', according to which decisions with consequences for the Church's universality should be made by the whole body of bishops meeting together on a regular basis. This model of decision-making is clearly based on the Second Vatican Council, but that he states was an event rather than an institution.[98] Bishops are able to make practical decisions collegially without assembling together in one place. To institute a regular council of bishops would risk replacing locally rooted collegiality with a centralized administrative apparatus.

De Lubac adopts a highly pragmatic approach to these and other elements of ecclesial administration and bureaucracy. They are useful but contingent, with their activities being in no way ends in themselves and not grounded in any self-validating source of authority. If points like these are not accepted by all participants in intermediate institutions, such institutions may in fact actively impair collegiality. There is quite simply 'no intermediary of a doctrinal order between the particular church and the universal Church'.[99] Collegiality 'greatly increases rather than reduces the personal responsibility and, consequently, the personal obligation of each pastor', yet 'sometimes seems to be confused with a sort of government of assemblies, commissions and committees' in which personal responsibility is actually resigned.[100] De Lubac hints that motherhood provides a possible alternative model for the exercise of responsibility in the Church that challenges practices based on bureaucratic rationality. It suggests a close, personal and irrevocable bond between the abstract theological role of nurturing the Church and the specific individual tasks essential to the successful and responsible completion of that ministry.

PRIESTHOOD AND PARENTHOOD

Priestly ordination derives from the universality of the Church, being a 'power received from Christ'.[101] De Lubac states unequivocally: 'In no case is it from the Christian people that these ministers hold their commission, nor, consequently, the authority necessary for its achievement. They are not an emanation from the priestly consciousness of the church. They are given to the church by the Father.'[102] Pastors are primarily representatives of God for the community, and only secondarily representatives before God of the community.[103] They are genuine leaders, and their ministry cannot be defined solely in terms of servanthood. The priest must accept the 'fact of being nearly always misunderstood'.[104]

Priesthood is focused above all in its liturgical dimension, which is for the sake of the whole Church, in which the priest prays and offers the Eucharist as the person of all but presides as the person of Christ, exercising power of consecration on behalf of the bishop.[105] The Eucharist reveals, moreover, some of the close connections between priesthood and motherhood. In the Eucharist, the Church 'carries out a sort of maternal function with regard to Christ himself',[106] bringing him to birth in the elements of bread and wine. Indeed, de Lubac suggests that Mary performs an exemplary priesthood in bringing Christ to birth in the world, providing an ideal for ordained priesthood and even its governing principle. She enjoys uniquely superior authority over the Church, being the living link between Church and Christ, and her coronation in heaven is already the coronation of the Church.[107] She is the 'unique case, the genuine universal concrete, which includes to an eminent degree and in a pure state the sum of perfection of all the other members' of the Church.[108]

The Church is not founded but born, and remains ceaselessly in the throes of giving birth.[109] The motherhood of the Church cannot, however, be directly equated with any sensible experience.[110] It does not follow, for instance, from the fact that because priesthood possesses a maternal dimension that it should be exercised by people who are biological mothers. De Lubac uses images drawn from material life as analogies, rather than literally, to describe the spiritual qualities of priestly ministry. Considering the relation between biological and spiritual parenthood in a purely practical way, it is far from clear that any natural progression exists from the first to the second, and that a harmful confusion of the two roles is just as likely to result from attempts to combine them. For example, a priest with young children might find it difficult to fulfil the equally demanding functions of biological and spiritual parenthood, whilst another with adult children might find it difficult to treat similarly aged members of his own congregation in an appropriately different way consonant with his relation to them as spiritual parent rather than biological parent. The tendency of married ministers of some denominations, on assuming a new appointment, to present themselves primarily as biological parents by means of large quantities of family biography demonstrates just how easily these two distinct roles can become confused and the spiritual essence of priesthood lost.

There is, despite this, no absolute opposition between marriage and priestly ordination. Yet there are several good reasons for the continued practice of clerical celibacy: the imitation of Christ, who was not a biological parent; total exterior and interior availability without the pressures and compelling demands of a biological family; and the fact that the priest exercises, in a derivative way, a 'paternal' function. In renouncing parenthood according to the flesh, the priest engenders numerous children according to the Spirit.[111] Moreover, if the priest is not a parent of biological children, it seems more likely that they will be able to become a spiritual parent in a way that combines images of paternity and maternity. Paul of Tarsus presents himself as both a spiritual father and spiritual mother, and the Church is described in theological meditation as both a maternal breast and a family.[112] Celibate clergy can, however, be deprived of the human need for close companionship which marriage provides, and so the community organization of priestly life is highly desirable.[113]

The clear distinction of biological paternity from spiritual paternity provides the possibility of creative dialectic between the two. De Lubac recounts the humility of a country priest described by Bernanos after conversing with a woman of village who showed him what paternity truly was.[114] From the perspective of the child, the relation between the two forms of parenthood is, indeed, paradoxical:

> Whereas, in the physical order, the child leaves the womb of his mother, and, withdrawing from her, becomes increasingly independent of her protective guardianship as he grows, becomes stronger and advances in years, the Church brings us forth to the new life she bears by receiving us into her womb, and the more our divine education progresses, the more we become intimately bound to her.[115]

As a result of marriage, mother and child are distinct, but in the Church, mother and child are one. It is through the intensification of this childlike spirit that the Christian 'advances to adulthood, penetrating ever deeper ... into the womb of his mother'.[116] Clement of Alexandria, in elaborating on this image, compares the Word to sacred milk on which the Church is nursed.[117] This imagery of the Christian as child contains, like that of the priest as father or mother, various possible practical consequences. It is no mere coincidence that images of spiritual childhood are rarely employed in church communities which tend to equate spiritual 'maturity' with the acquisition of a stock of personal experience of what is termed 'real life'. The image of spiritual childhood suggests, of course, a reversed order of priority, according to which cultural, sociological and psychological experience is recognized as dependent on the revelation of the God who gives birth to the whole of creation. Experience needs to be adapted to the essential requirements which this revelation provides.

THE MISSION OF THE CHURCH

The function of the Church is to continue the redemptive mission of God in Christ through the Spirit to the world. The Church 'completes – so far as can be completed here below – the work of spiritual reunion which was made necessary by sin; that work which was begun at the Incarnation and was carried on up to Calvary'.[118] It is the 'permanent witness of Christ and the messenger of the living God',[119] and called, unlike any other body either on earth or in heaven, to make Christ present to humankind.[120] It is the body to which the Word of God is addressed, and for this reason the body in which that Word is heard and proclaimed.[121] The Gospel is never-theless announced primarily not in word but through living: 'It is by living by Christ's Spirit that the Church manifests him and spreads his name abroad.'[122] Thus the history of the Church's missions *is* the history of the Church.[123] Notable is de Lubac's view that the saving work of Christ begins with his incarnation rather than with his passion or death, which he sees in contrast as being continuations and intensifications of the incarnation. He conceives the Church's unifying work in the world in the widest possible terms. It 'includes all the host of angels and even extends to the whole of the cosmos as well', and is in principle bound by no limits in space or time. Three groups may be distinguished in the Church in ceaseless communica-tion with one other: the Church militant in this world, the Church suffering in purgatory, and the Church triumphant in heaven. These distinctions mirror the trinitarian terms in which Christ has spoken about himself and revealed himself to humankind as Father, Son and Holy Spirit, the single, living God.[124]

Participation in the Church is the essential vocation of individual Christians. This is because credal affirmations, liturgy, missionary activity and work of reconciliation form, express, preserve and transmit the Christian faith. De Lubac declares:

> It is the Church that believes. It is she who confesses the Trinity, she who offers praise and thanksgiving; it is she who hopes and awaits the return of her Lord, she who bears witness to him by her unfailing faith which bears fruit throughout the world. It is she who, advancing in faith, prays and works, seeking in all things to fulfil the divine will. It is she whom the Spirit of Christ gathers into one and unifies; she whom he enlightens and guides throughout her long earthly pilgrimage. It is she who, while awaiting the face-to-face vision, faithful amidst trials and dark-ness, resisting all scandal, jealously preserves the deposit entrusted to her. For every one of us, the Church is the archetype of the perfect 'yes'.[125]

There is, de Lubac repeatedly insists, no private Christianity.[126] Membership of the Church and participation in its visible institutions make possible a faith rooted in the ambiguous nature of concrete living which will contribute to the redemption of that nature. The Church does not serve as an intermediary between God and the believer, but as the body in whom and through whom God 'gives himself immediately to the one who believes in him'.[127] This is why Christians say the Creed together yet using the singular form: not 'We believe in God' but 'I believe in God'.[128]

In defending the various concrete elements of religion, de Lubac regards them as ends in themselves which nevertheless serve a higher spiritual purpose. Christians are not called to sit in judgement on the tradition which has been passed on to them, and without which they would possess no knowledge of Christ. Equally, the transient human interpretation of this tradition in particular times and places is necessarily incomplete and vulnerable to fetishization. Mission therefore consists not in inculcating people into a set of rituals and practices but in presenting people in uplifted hands to God:

> If it is at once understood that the work of conversion consists, fundamentally, not in adapting supernatural truth, in bringing it down to human level, but, on the contrary, in adapting humanity to it, raising humanity up to the truth that rules and judges it, we must especially beware, as of blasphemy, of confusing ourselves, its servants, with it – ourselves, our tastes, our habits, our prejudices, our passions, our narrow-mindedness and our weaknesses with the divine religion with which we are so little imbued. We must give souls to God, not conquer them for ourselves.[129]

It is in this sense that de Lubac cites with approval the statement of the *Shepherd of Hermas* that God created the world for the Church.[130] This perspective applies Israel's understanding of its identity to the Church.[131] The purpose of a chosen people is not to preserve religious and cultural exclusivity but precisely the opposite: to prepare the whole of humankind for fellowship with God and to draw it into that promised fellowship. This eschatological vision enables de Lubac to affirm that 'definitively the Church is nothing else than humanity itself, enlivened, unified by the Spirit of Christ.'[132]

In light perhaps of the intrinsically ambivalent character of actual church practice, de Lubac regards the Church's mission fields with great respect, specifically rejecting the notion pervasive in much current theology that the 'modern age has experienced outside the church only error and decadence'.[133] He is not a stock critic of 'modernity'. In an intricately interlinked global society and economy, Christians are continually dependent on people of no religion, and of other religions, for their basic material needs and greater flourishing. This global perspective, in which individual identity is undermined, gives new meaning to the patristic vision of humanity as a single whole, and not specific individuals, as the being to whom salvation is ultimately offered:

> As 'unbelievers' are, in the design of providence, indispensable for building the body of Christ, they must in their own way profit from their vital connection with this same body. By an extension of the dogma of the communion of saints, it seems right to think that though they themselves are not in the normal way of salvation, they will be able nevertheless to obtain this salvation by virtue of those mysterious bonds which unite them to the faithful. In short, they can be saved because they are an integral part of that humanity which is to be saved.[134]

From earliest times the Church was regarded as being, in a certain sense, 'nothing else than the human race itself, in all the phases of its history, in so far as it was to lead to Christ and be quickened by his spirit. It was the entire human condition.'[135] The missionary task is to bring all people to a more explicit acknowledgment of their participation in the mystical body of Christ.

CHAPTER FOUR

SCRIPTURE

Littera gesta docet, quid credas allegoria,
Moralis quid agas, quo tendas anagogia.

The letter teaches what took place, the allegory what to believe,
the moral what to do, the anagogy what goal to strive for.[1]

De Lubac employs this pithy couplet to outline the doctrine of the
'fourfold sense' of Scripture. In so doing, he wishes to reappropriate
a fundamentally theological and synthetic mode of scriptural
reading. This was prominent in the precritical era but has more
recently been occluded by scientific methods of division and analysis borrowed from other fields of knowledge like history and literature.[2] Exegesis should not, he argues, be conceived as a critical
discipline which approaches the text inquisitorially, but as a path of
learning guided by the text. This is because theology is grounded in
the revelation of God in Christ through Scripture. Indeed theology
(or sacred doctrine) is, as Aquinas makes clear in the opening question of his *Summa theologiae*, no more than the sacred reading and
exposition of Scripture.[3] The origins of these various activities are
liturgical: proclamation and preaching.[4]

De Lubac seeks to establish that the fourfold sense is the method of
scriptural reading which conforms to the content of revelation which
Scripture reveals. His hermeneutic thus emerges from Scripture rather
than being developed independently of Scripture and then applied on
to it. The fourfold sense is therefore peculiar to Scripture, being its
'unique privilege'.[5] The historical method de Lubac employs to
recover this method of scriptural reading itself points, as always in his
work, to a fundamental interpretive principle: the tradition of reading

Scripture has been handed down to present-day readers and should provide the basis for their own reading. The notion that Scripture can be read, or is read, in a historical vacuum is no more feasible than the view that reason or language are formed by nothing more than a dialogue among the people currently alive in the world.

SCRIPTURAL QUESTIONING

How should followers of Christ ask questions about the Scriptures which speak of him? There is a widespread type of historical-critical exegesis which, de Lubac suggests, focuses excessively on the literal sense, and presumes that it is on this sense that the meaning of Scripture depends. His immediate target is the nineteenth-century 'quest of the historical Jesus', which applied critical method to scriptural texts in order to recover the 'true' person of Jesus shorn of metaphysical claims. This was, however, just the most recent iteration of a more ancient tendency. De Lubac traces the origins of critical method to the beginning of the thirteenth century with the rise of academic learning which followed the birth of the first major European universities in Bologna and Paris. These developments were in turn bound up with the rise of Aristotelian dialectic and disputation – a method exemplified in the work of figures like Peter Abelard and Peter Lombard. Peter Cantor complains that 'modern' theologians such as these were more concerned with spreading snares for others that with discerning the truth. Their questioning is, therefore, *bad* questioning, and a distraction from the search for wisdom which is the commission of every follower of Christ.[6] Above all, such questioning silences the questions that Scripture is posing to humankind.[7]

In monasteries, where the reading of Scripture was rooted in prayer and meditation, Scripture itself shaped the community in which it was read.[8] In the Rule of Benedict, which provided the model for later monastic constitutions, the communal pattern of daily worship and living are modelled on Scripture. This is equally true of the essential elements of the monastic vocation enumerated in the prologue: to hear the word of God, pursue goodness, and live a life of faith, action and repentance. Wisdom about a whole range of more practical matters is also drawn from Scripture: governance, obedience, silence, humility, and even the times of prayer and character of the kitchen manager.[9] The image of Ruth gleaning ears of corn left by the harvesters in the field provides an analogy for the attentive searching of Scripture for spiritual truth in which exegetes like Benedict engaged.[10]

Universities challenged the monopoly on learning which religious houses had previously enjoyed. The new approaches of dialectic and disputation that they encouraged set up obstacles to contemplation, de Lubac protests, and when pursued brings contentious questions storming into Scripture.[11] Quarrels, controversies, and conflicts certainly have the potential to provide the catalyst for progress in theological understanding. Yet during the twelfth century, he argues, questions became multiplied, and were posed less as part of the exploration of the mystery of faith in humility, admiration and wonderment, and more in an attempt to establish a body of scientifically proven facts. Questions were perceived everywhere, being the 'product of idle and undisciplined minds or minds that sought to push themselves into the vanguard'.[12] Modern examples of such questioning include entrapment questioning, and frivolous or obscure questions designed primarily to impress others, especially the less intellectually able, or simply to perpetuate intellectual activity. Dialectical questioning has often belied weakness of faith because it has not been firmly grounded in the mystery and contingencies of belief.

De Lubac wishes, as part of his 'critique of criticism',[13] to challenge the opinion of many pagan philosophers that Scripture presents, due to its crude language, teaching suited only to the simple and uneducated. Even Augustine, while a student at Carthage, considered its Koine peasant dialect 'unworthy to be compared to the dignity of Cicero'.[14] His mature assessment of course shows him esteeming Scripture as highly as de Lubac, and censorious of his former arrogance:

> Something neither open to the proud nor laid bare to mere children; a text lowly to the beginner but, on further reading, of mountainous difficulty and enveloped in mysteries . . . My inflated conceit shunned the Bible's restraint, and my gaze never penetrated to its inwardness. Yet the Bible was composed in such a way that as beginners mature, its meaning grows with them. I disdained to be a little beginner. Puffed up with pride, I considered myself a mature adult.[15]

Intellectual enlightenment is the product of Scripture and contained within it. This is particularly true of the classic liberal arts of grammar, rhetoric, logic, arithmetic, music, geometry and astronomy. De Lubac insists that these emerge from Scripture rather than from other secular sources. As Rupert of Deutz states: 'Those who have examined the scriptures by way of wisdom are amazed to make the discovery not only that these arts were always there, but also that they were so hidden, so obscured by the light and the majesty of mistress wisdom, that it was not easy to see that they were there.'[16] The belief that philosophy and culture emerge from Scripture has at certain times been justified by the myth of the 'Attic Moses' – that Moses was taught Platonist philosophy during his captivity in Egypt – and the theory that Greek philosophers were taught by Abraham. Such histories now appear fanciful if accepted in their literal sense, but their motivating intuition is sound. Philosophy and theology are inalienably conjoined, as Clement of Alexandria affirms in his *Stromata*: 'As the encyclical branches of study contribute to philosophy, which is their mistress, so also philosophy itself co-operates for the acquisition of wisdom. For philosophy is the study of wisdom, and wisdom is the knowledge of things divine and human; and their causes.'[17] The history of European painting, sculpture, architecture, music and literature provides ample evidence in support of this claim. The evolving canon of European culture is synchronous with the history of reflection on the truths about Christ revealed in Scripture. Moreover, the visual arts show that it is the images and narrative of Scripture which inspire the imagination to represent the truths of faith, rather than the doctrinal formulae derived from those truths, whether from the studios of Giotto, Michelangelo and Picasso, or William Blake and Graham Sutherland.

THE HISTORICAL SENSE AND THE LITERAL SENSE

Scripture gives, at its most basic level, an account of events and interpretation of those events. In a paper presented in 1948, de Lubac states:

> Literally the scripture gives us facts. It tells us about things that actually happened. It is neither a dissertation of abstract doctrine nor a collection of myths. The divine revelation has a historical form; religion is first of all a historical fact. God has intervened in human history: the first thing to do is to learn the history of his

interventions from the book where they have been recorded by the Holy Spirit.[18]

De Lubac subsequently unfolds a distinction between two types of narrative. One describes events in Scripture presented as historical facts, such as the Babylonian captivity, the birth of Christ, and the preaching of the apostles in Acts. The other, which includes the proverbs, and the parables narrated by Christ, refers to real life events but does not claim that the events presented actually took place. In other words, the whole of Scripture is historically true, but not all of it is literally true.

This contrast provides the basis for de Lubac's distinction between the historical and literal senses of Scripture. The whole of Scripture possesses, he argues, an *historical* sense. Every passage is historic in the sense of containing, in the words of Isidore of Seville, a 'simple expression that is understood just as it is said'.[19] The narrative could, in other words, be a true description of events, and is in any case not meaningless. The historical sense thus refers simply to the fact that Scripture always makes use of meaningful symbols and concepts. Even in Daniel and Revelations, where particular images are sometimes employed in strange contexts or combinations, they remain comprehensible. Not all parts of Scripture have a *literal* sense, however, because not all provide information about events which have actually taken place. Parts of the two books just cited are good examples. This terminological distinction may be grasped more easily in the French, where an '*histoire*' is simply a story. In English an inverse relation between meaning and fact is implied, with *literature* rather than history providing the possibility of an account of events which have not in fact taken place.

The contrast is not, however, purely etymological, because it raises large questions about the meaning and scope of the term 'history'. De Lubac reminds his readers that history possesses both objective and subjective connotations, as suggested by the derivation of the concept from *isterion*, i.e. seeing and gesturing.[20] All historical narrative therefore includes an element of histrionics: history comprises both the 'deeds recounted' and the 'report of these deeds'. It is in this sense that history provides the universal foundation of scriptural interpretation. The truth of history cannot ultimately be measured against 'objective' criteria, for what other criteria could there be apart from those selected and announced by another interpreter? The validity of the history recounted in Scripture is instead rooted in the depth, power and coherence of its narrative and its capacity to bring people to faith in Christ. Once this point is accepted, the history of Scripture then becomes the standard of truth against which other particular histories are measured.

The historical sense of Scripture provides the foundations for all its other senses. At the same time, the historical sense depends on each of the others for the full expression of its meaning because the whole of history is Christ-centred. The historical sense employs narrative principles according to which events are selected and located within a texture of succession and causation governed by the action of God in Christ on the world. Questions about which parts of Scripture are *literally* true – with the implication being that this is all that matters – miss the fundamental point that the truth of scriptural reading depends on the extent to which the four senses combine in each describing a part of God's revelation in Christ.

THE SPIRITUAL SENSE AND THE MYSTICAL SENSE

The fourfold sense of Scripture is a development of a single bipolar distinction of the spiritual sense of Scripture from its literal sense. The four different senses are therefore not each equivalent refractions of the other three. Rather, the historical sense is reflected in each of the other three senses in combination, which together comprise the spiritual sense.[21] The fourfold distinction is

> merely a development from the formula in two terms which is the essential, primitive formula which remains the permanent one. It is, let us remark, not obtained at the cost of adding new elements, taking them on in series, but, organically, by analysis of the second term and breaking it down into three parts. Here everything comes from the hiatus which had to exist from the first day, between the two comings of Christ.[22]

Scripture refers historically to Christ's incarnation and earthly ministry. It also refers to his second coming, prepared at Pentecost by the sending of the Holy Spirit on his disciples. Thus the twofold distinction is, like the others, defined by the saving action of Christ for the world. It would of course be alien to de Lubac's method to develop abstract principles for interpreting Scripture and then to apply them like tools to the texts. He envisions the principles for interpreting Scripture as emerging from Scripture itself in an enlightenment governed by the action of Christ who is the subject of Scripture. De Lubac depicts illumination via the three other senses by means of a Trinitarian motif: allegory, which speaks of the humanity of the Word and relates to the Son; tropology, which concerns spiritual life and refers to the Holy Spirit; and anagogy, which raises the intellect to contemplate divinity and reflects the Father.[23] He later delineates an overtly Christological scheme of correspondence within a 'threefold advent': the humble and hidden work of redemption pursued in the Church and her sacraments, which are the body of Christ; the interior advent unfolded within the soul of every follower of Christ; and the third advent which is saved up for the end times when Christ will return in glory.[24]

Spiritual interpretation of Scripture is sometimes regarded with suspicion because it is thought to undermine Scripture's historical sense. De Lubac does not accept this opposition, believing in contrast that the spiritual sense is dependent on the literal sense. The spiritual sense 'does not eliminate the literal sense or add something else to it but rather rounds it out and gives it its fullness, revealing its depths and bringing out its objective extension'.[25] The spiritual senses would be redundant if they did not describe a given historical reality inhabited by both Christ and humanity: they are valid precisely because they explain the wider significance and meaning of that reality. That the raising of Lazarus prefigures Christ's resurrection and thus conveys a spiritual meaning does not, for instance, contradict the fact that Lazarus was raised from the dead. Equally, when Augustine states that many passages of Scripture ought to be read not literally but figuratively, the examples he offers show that 'this manner of understanding them presupposed the recognition of their historical sense'.[26] One of the illustrations Augustine uses is the salvation history of Israel exemplified in concrete events like the passage through the Red Sea and the feeding with manna in the wilderness.[27] His understanding of the historical character of the history of the people of Israel is thus identical to Paul's: 'These things happened to them to serve as an example, and they were written down to instruct us, on whom the ends of the ages have come.'[28]

The spiritual sense is necessary for the completion of the historical, whilst the historical sense is the indispensable foundation of the spiritual: '*The spirit is not outside the history*. They are given together, inseparably, through the fact of a single inspiration. It is we who, after the event, separate them . . . *once the time has come*, on the Saviour's order and in imitation of him.'[29] The fragmentation of the senses is effected by human intellect, and not a property inherent in Scripture itself. De Lubac here employs a eucharistic analogy: just as Christ is revealed in the breaking of bread, so the breaking up of Scripture into different senses makes possible Christ's revelation of himself to human understanding in the Word. It is only by means of the breaking that sacramental unity may be attained in Church and world.

Just as the historical sense and the literal sense are often considered synonymous, but in fact possess more precise distinct meanings, so the subtle difference between the spiritual sense and the mystical sense must also be appreciated. Mystery, de Lubac states, 'carries a strongly objective connotation, more specifically objective than "spirit"'.[30] The mystical sense is the 'sense related to the mystery, which is a reality, at first hidden in God, and then revealed to human beings at the same time as realized in Jesus Christ', and therefore the 'sense which contains the plenitude of the doctrine'. He states:

> Mystery is entirely concrete. It does not exist in idea. It does not consist in any atemporal truth or object of detached speculation. This mystery is a reality in act, the realization of a Grand Design; it is therefore, in the strongest sense, even something historical, in which personal beings are engaged.[31]

Mystery is therefore sacramental, being the 'interior component, the reality hidden under the letter and signified by the sign, the truth that the figure indicates; in other words, the object of faith itself'.[32] It is for this reason that Augustine is able to describe the Scriptures as the 'books of the divine sacraments'. De Lubac implies that in the fracturing of the twofold distinction between the historical sense and the spiritual sense, by means of the internal differentiation of the latter, spiritual understanding is deepened such that it becomes a mystical appreciation of the concrete truths of faith.

THE ALLEGORICAL SENSE

Allegory has often been contested as an alien method of reading Scripture imported into early Christianity from classical Greek paganism. De Lubac is determined to refute this 'invincible misunderstanding of the essential meaning that it takes on in the exegetical tradition'.[33] He traces the origins of allegorical method of scriptural reading to shortly before the birth of Jesus, suggesting that its advent was in fact bound up with the coming of Christ into the world. Use of allegory is, moreover, endorsed by the substantial authority of Paul, who expounds one Old Testament episode explicitly in this way: the birth of the sons of Abraham by Hagar and Sarah.[34] Hagar, a slave woman, bears children according to the old covenant of the law and the flesh, whilst Sarah, the free woman, gives birth to children corresponding to the heavenly Jerusalem, and is thus the mother of believers in Christ, who are set free from the law. Paul states: 'This is an allegory: these women are two covenants. One woman, in fact, is Hagar, from Mount Sinai, bearing children for slavery. Now Hagar is Mount Sinai in Arabia and corresponds to the present Jerusalem, for she is in slavery with her children. But the other woman corresponds to the Jerusalem above; she is free, and she is our mother.'[35]

True allegory could not be further removed from the efforts of nineteenth-century source critics like David Strauss to present foundational elements of the historical Gospel narratives, such as Christ's resurrection, as mere myths.[36] Allegory is not a transposition of historical facts into a realm of mythical significance, but the universalization and intensification of those facts by drawing out their implications for current life. De Lubac states:

> The letter that is rejected is that of carnal observances; a letter that the grace of Christ has definitively changed in the spiritual sense and in Christian liberty; a letter of an outdated Testament, which no longer carries the spirit, which no longer promises it; a letter to which he who denies the Gospel, in his blindness, is bound; a letter which no longer has any 'hidden virtue', since it has already borne its fruit. It is, in other words, the letter sterilized. This letter kills, because it is itself dead.[37]

Faith in Christ cannot be lived out by the unspiritual observance of legal requirements. The law has not been rendered obsolete, however, but given a new deeper significance and fulfilment by Christ that is expressed allegorically. By means of allegorical interpretation, a shift or transformation is achieved in which is resolved the conflict that has become inevitable between the letter of that which is held to be normative and the demands of the new intellectual and moral situation. Thus new problems receive an appropriate solution, and progress can be welcomed without the sacred bond being broken and without an alteration of the fervent attachment to venerable teachings or prescriptions.[38]

This perspective of completion rather than supersession is especially significant for Christian understanding of Hebrew Scripture, in which de Lubac finds a vast store of allegory which points to Christ and is completed and understood in him. In a pamphlet published in 1942, de Lubac states: 'The God of Jesus is the God of the prophets, who concludes by revealing himself. Jesus has not come to reject but to carry out the heart of the message of which the people of Israel were the bearer.'[39]

Allegory both assumes different forms and admits a plurality of interpretations. In Scripture it appears variously as anthropomorphisms, such as a person encountering God whilst strolling in a garden in the cool of the evening; messianic prophecies, as evoked by the wolf grazing with the lamb; precepts presented under an imagined form, among them plucking out one's right eye if it motivates sin; the exterior dramatization of a spiritual fact, for instance the man Jesus seeing with human eyes all the kingdoms of the world during his temptation by the devil.[40] The meaning of allegory is equivocal, but this in no way undermines the fundamental truth of faith.[41] Its equivocity is due to the limitations of human understanding and not to any deficiency of revelation.

Such a wide range of allegorical style and meanings may be retained within a single whole because coherence is dependent not on the expression of facts but on the facts which are themselves imperfectly expressed. Both critics and proponents of allegory are wrong to see it as fragmenting the fundamental unity of Scripture. De Lubac affirms: 'Allegory is not a means to which one should have recourse with a view of getting oneself off the hook; it can, on the contrary, be a means of explaining events from God's point of view, i.e., of corroborating them.'[42] The focal object of allegory is the 'divinity of the Word of God incarnate',[43] in other words the action of God in the world. Its meaning is therefore situated not in the text but in events:

To discover this allegory, one will not find it properly speaking in the text, but in the realities of which the text speaks; not in history as recitation, but in history as event; or, if one wishes, allegory is indeed in the recitation, but one that relates a real event. 'The actions speak . . . The deeds, if you understand them, are words.' Allegory is prophecy inscribed within the facts themselves . . . The text acts only as spokesman to lead to the historical realities; the latter are themselves the figures, they themselves contain the mysteries that the exercise of allegory is supposed to extract from them.[44]

Thus 'Scripture is in a way doubly the word of God, since God speaks to us in it with words about what he has spoken to us in deeds.'[45] Allegory is therefore intrinsically related to faith, and teaches belief. In order to penetrate into the cellar where its wines are tasted, it is necessary first to pass through the gate of faith.[46] The unity of Scripture is thus provided by Christ's revelation recognized and assented to by faith.

Allegory helps to explain the reason for the presence in Scripture of evil or deeply sinful episodes, such as Lot's fathering of sons by his own daughters and David's manslaughter of Uriah in order to take his wife Bathsheba as his own wife.[47] Such narratives reveal allegorically something about the action of God's redeeming providence in reprehensible chains of events. De Lubac reflects:

In stating such facts, Scripture does not approve of them: it leaves the judgement of them to our conscience enlightened by the divine law. But to grasp its intention, we shall recall that the whole Old Testament has value as prophecy, and in looking for the significance of all that it contains, we will justify Scripture without defending human sins . . . We must marvel that [God] puts to divine use even the weaknesses of his own people.[48]

This exercise is termed 'antiphrasis', or inverted signification, and appropriates Pseudo-Dionysius's notion of 'metaphors without likeness' closely allied with negative theology.[49] We can gain understanding of God by reflecting on what God is *not* like as well as on what God *is* like.

De Lubac warns against allowing interpretation of Scripture to develop excessive hardness and rigidity.[50] Allegory suggests an opposing dynamic, being by nature impossible to control. It can be depicted with the apophatic images of shadows, darkness, night, mist and clouds enshrouding the mystery.[51] Another possibility is the ecstatic imagery from the Song of Solomon: the Word hiding himself and then allowing a glimpse of him to be seen, before bounding off across the mountains and hiding in the valleys: 'He comes, approaches, then retires forthwith. He shows himself for an instant only to stir up desire. His furtive visits seem like unkept promises.'[52] This ongoing exegetical search refuses the temptation of Mary Magdalen, which was not her desire and longing for the truth of the Word, but the wish to touch and possess him.

THE TROPOLOGICAL SENSE: MORAL AND MYSTICAL

A trope is a 'figure, a mode, or a turn of phrase, by which one turns some expression to designate some object other than the one naturally meant'.[53] Tropology is speech turned around, or in its more developed form, speech which turns (something else) around. The tropological sense of Scripture can be described as moral because it performs this function of conversion or edification. It should not, however, be understood as moral simply in the sense of being concerned with detailed normative prescriptions for human action. De Lubac states: 'We pass from history to tropology through allegory.'[54] He thus opposes a long theological tradition extending from Origen and Clement of Alexandria through to Peter Lombard and his contemporaries according to which the moral sense must be taught, meditated on and internalized prior to the allegorical one.[55] He complains: 'Morality, indeed Christian morality, was placed ahead of the mystery upon which it in fact depended.'[56]

De Lubac is usually deeply appreciative of patristic tradition, but here makes a conscious departure from it. Virtue does not provide the path to faith, he argues, but faith the possibility of a virtuous life. The question of whether allegory or tropology comes first is to some degree abstract: medieval interpretation frequently passed in practice through one sense to another in no uniform order of succession, and the senses are in any case not systematically demarcated.[57] Nevertheless, the issue of whether moral interpretation emerges directly from a historical reading of Scripture or is mediated by an allegorical one is decisive in shaping responses to questions affecting the order and life of the Church and its relation to wider society. In particular, approaches which admit to allegory a role in shaping interpretation are usually more sensitive to human experience and inculturation, both in ecclesiological questions and moral issues, than ones which seek to pass immediately from a historical and literal reading of Scripture to principles of practical morality.

De Lubac suggests, in fact, that the moral sense both precedes the allegorical and is dependent on it, delineating a 'twofold tropology' comprising one type that 'unites us to Christ by charity' and its corollary which 'joins the soul with the spirit'.[58] In drawing this distinction, he employs an analogy based on his tripartite definition of the person as comprised of body, soul and spirit:

> On the one hand, a moral sense obtains, and this, coming as it does immediately after the letter or the 'body' of scripture, corresponds to the 'soul' and precedes the sense which acts as the carrier of 'spirit'. On the other hand, the moral sense which prolongs and presupposes the allegorical or mystical sense is properly speaking 'spiritual'.[59]

This analogy is not wholly arbitrary, because the different senses of Scripture themselves relate to different aspects of human understanding. This is part of de Lubac's wider analogical cosmology: when God shows himself to humanity, his revelation structures and is structured by the human understanding which receives it, with visible creation and Scripture functioning as two organically related revelations.[60] Scripture is needed in order to understand creation, but in so doing speaks of the goodness and value of creation and of its coherence as a realm capable of being described and understood by human language and reason.

The first form of tropology is *natural* and draws moral lessons from Scripture 'in the same way that any datum of literature, humanity, and the universe can be moralized'.[61] This could reasonably be described as moral tropology, but is as such not distinctively Christian. Moral readings of Scripture that are directly and solely reliant on the historical or literal senses are by no means somehow purer or closer to the truth than those employing allegory. De Lubac in fact regards allegory and not history as the uniquely Christian method of interpreting Scripture. An entirely literal reading would provide no information beyond a simple description of events which occurred and teaching given in a particular time and place. As soon as any attempt is made to infer theological implications for present-day Church or society, the allegorical sense is inevitably employed, even when unacknowledged.

The second form of tropology is *mystical*, contributing to the spiritual sense of Scripture by augmenting its meaning and exerting itself 'within it to complete it' as part of an allegorical progression. De Lubac declares of this mystical tropology:

> It is within allegory. It constitutes an integral part of the mystery. Coming after the objective aspect of which it is the allegory, it constitutes its subjective aspect. It is, if one can say so, its intussusception, its interiorization; it appropriates it for us . . . If allegory, starting from the facts of history, envisions the mystical body in its head or in its totality, tropology envisions it in each of its members.[62]

A key characteristic of tropology is that it addresses the individual subject. It should not therefore be regarded as inferior to allegory, but as the translation of allegory into principles with consequences for concrete reality. Tropology provides the means by which humanity is brought to perfection, in conjunction with its nourishment on history and growth by means of allegory.[63] De Lubac insists:

> In this Christian soul, it is each day, it is today, that the mystery, by being interiorized, is accomplished . . . Each day, deep within ourselves, Israel departs from Egypt; each day, it is nourished with manna; each day the promises that had been made to this people under a bodily form are realized spiritually in us . . . After his coming on earth, Jesus must also come into each soul, so as to overturn the idols within it, to conquer Babylon within, the city of the devil . . . Christ must once again be conceived and formed in each soul, so that the great joy may be renewed as many times as the angels have announced it of old.[64]

Scripture is thus presented to humanity like a mirror in which the life of the soul in search of God is reflected. De Lubac states:

> In this mirror we learn to know our nature and our destiny; in it we also see the different stages through which we have passed since creation, the beautiful and the ugly features of our internal

face. It shows us the truth of our being by pointing it out in its relation to the Creator. It is a living mirror, a living and efficacious Word, a sword penetrating at the juncture of soul and spirit, which makes our secret thoughts appear and reveals to us our heart. It teaches us to read in the book of experience and makes us, so to speak, our own exegesis.[65]

Material life is in this sense the Word speaking itself. There is ultimately no distinction between the meaning of concrete life and the narrative of Scripture: 'real life' is described by Scripture, whilst Scripture is a product of that life.

Moral tropology is therefore subsumed within mystical tropology once tropology as a whole is seen to be rooted in the action of Christ, who is the immediate exemplar of all personal life:

> Since Christ's deeds in truth, in the depth of the mystery, realize what the facts of biblical history prefigured, when one takes one's point of departure from within these actions of Christ one will no longer have to count three steps but only two, and from history – which is now already more than mere history – one will pass directly to tropology.[66]

Tropology, being the sense of Scripture in which it is 'fully *for us* the Word of God, this Word which is addressed to each person',[67] calls the hearer and reader of Scripture to a conversion of the heart and the restoration of the divine image within her soul. This conversion is expressed in charity, which is a more apt word than 'love' in so far as it suggests a concrete dimension rooted in the pursuit of justice and equity by means of concrete action. Charity is more than a sentiment of diffuse benevolence: 'It is in charity that tropology shows itself to allegory in interior perfection: for the perfection of the Law is charity and it is at the same time the Christ.'[68]

THE ANAGOGICAL (ESCHATOLOGICAL) SENSES

De Lubac identifies a 'twofold anagogy', one part of which fulfils the doctrinal formulation of the fourfold sense and the other the threefold spiritual formulation.[69] *Both* form equally and from the beginning part of the mystical sense, in contrast with tropology, where only the mystical element of its twofold character may be incorporated directly into a spiritual reading of Scripture. The first anagogy teaches the objective doctrine of eschatology, which concerns the ultimate ends of individual persons and the whole universe. The second anagogy draws the person of faith into the contemplative mystical life.

The anagogical perspective is one of the *interim*, in which the 'very reality of salvation . . . is inserted in history and immediately offered to us' so that the person of faith has 'already, albeit secretly, penetrated into the kingdom'.[70] The interim is within time, but shows that 'time must ultimately lead to what no longer belongs to time'.[71] This does not require a passage from time into eternity in the sense of an 'escape into the atemporal' but the assigning to history of a term which no longer belongs to it but which grants its final role and value. In anagogical perspective, moral action does not therefore simply prepare for the coming of the heavenly kingdom, but actually builds that kingdom. The anagogical sense of Scripture that reveals this fact thus completes a unique synthesizing and teleological function:

> Anagogy realizes the perfection both of allegory and of tropology, achieving their synthesis. It is neither 'objective' like the first, nor 'subjective' like the second. Above and beyond this division, it realizes their unity. It integrates the whole and final meaning. It sees, in eternity, the fusion of the mystery and the mystic. In other words, the eschatological reality attained by anagogy is the eternal reality within which every other has its consummation.[72]

The fourfold sense of Scripture is unified in eschatology, which presents a fulfilment, but one that is a promised hope rather than fully realized in present human life. Anagogy 'stirs up the desire for eternity in us'.[73] Because it shows to human life its ultimate finality, anagogy is the last of the senses of Scripture, being dependent on the senses preceding it and necessarily concluding their succession. It nevertheless suffers from an 'incurable' and 'fatal' incompleteness that needs to be 'considered above all in its positive and dynamic aspect', sustained by the action of the Spirit which 'communicates to it a virtuality without limits'.[74] This transcendent dimension of eschatology expands both the world and the understanding of the God who interprets it.

Proper evaluation of the eschatological sense is vital, de Lubac argues, because it prevents the spiritual interpretation becoming focused solely concerned on private inner contemplation.[75] The corollary of this inward turn would be a 'darkening of social and eschatological perspective' which loses sight of the social and political eschatology delineated so strikingly in John's Revelation.[76] It is essential that the reading of Scripture remain both within the world and for the world.

CHRIST THE NEW TESTAMENT

In his scriptural exegesis, de Lubac frequently emphasizes the continuity between the Old and New Testaments. 'The New Testament,' he states, 'is the fruit of a supernatural tree whose roots and trunks and leaves were the Old Testament.'[77] It perfects, fulfils and transfigures the Old, which lives on within it.[78] He is particularly insistent on this point in some of his wartime writing as part of his practical efforts to combat anti-Semitism.[79]

De Lubac emphasizes the real, absolute dependence of the New Covenant on the Old. The sacraments of the New Covenant emerge in early Christian tradition as functions of their types. For instance, the offering by Melchizedek, the sending of the manna to the Israelites in the wilderness, and the Temple shewbread, provide both the idea and the historical origin of the Eucharist.[80] There exist an 'inherent continuity' and 'ontological bond' between the Eucharist and its preceding facts 'due to the same divine will which is active in both situations and which, from stage to stage, is pursuing a single Design'.[81] De Lubac is here inspired by the letter to the Hebrews, which presents a close intrinsic relation between the two Testaments.[82]

The two Testaments are nevertheless divided by a rupture, which establishes an 'infinite qualitative difference' between them.[83] De Lubac describes Paul's first letter to the Thessalonians, usually reckoned as the earliest composition of the New Testament, as an 'unparalleled innovation in human history' in which 'everything has reference to the person of Jesus, everything originates in the event of Jesus'.[84] The Old Testament foreshadows Christ, whereas the New reveals Christ himself. The New Testament is therefore self-sufficient once it is announced, whereas the Old depends on that which follows for its full meaning, remaining in itself intrinsically incomplete. De Lubac affirms:

Truth itself is present in the New Testament, though it can be perceived only as a reflection. The New Testament will never date; it is of its very nature the Testament that never grows old, the last and newest Testament. It should therefore be interpreted – as far as possible while we are still in this world – in accordance with those principles that are laid down in it; whereas the Old Testament, beyond the facts and events which the literal meaning of the text teaches us, designates also 'something else' that very reality of which (not merely the manifestation of it) is to come.[85]

The key to interpreting the whole sweep of scriptural narrative, in both Testaments and according to its various senses previously delineated, is God's revelation of himself in a form perfectly congruent with human understanding:

One is led by a series of singular facts up to one other singular fact; one series of divine interventions, whose reality itself is significant, leads to another sort of divine intervention, equally real, but deeper and more decisive. Everything culminates in one great fact, which, in its unique singularity, has multiple repercussions; which dominates history and which is the bearer of all light as well as of all spiritual fecundity: *the fact of Christ*.[86]

The 'reverberation of this great fact' is evident through the subsequent history of the mystical interpretation of Scripture. It is unique because it happens 'only once in time', but also because it 'alone among all facts, was prefigured by the long series of facts in the old covenant'.[87]

Christ is nevertheless the completion of the tradition rather than its contradiction or abolition. Christ is the 'end of history'.[88] In the words of Aelred of Rievaulx, 'Our Lord Jesus Christ suddenly emerged in the clear from the thickest forest of allegorical words, in whose dark density he was hitherto concealed.'[89] The revelation of God in Christ had been prepared through many generations and several covenants: from Adam to Noah, Noah to Moses, Moses to David, and David to John the Baptist, in a progression of 'successive spiritualizations'. These extended into the ministry of Christ, which in Luke's Gospel is inaugurated by his own exposition of Isaiah, and continue beyond his resurrection in his exposition of the 'things about himself' contained in the law of Moses, the prophets and the Psalms to his disciples on the Emmaus road and in Jerusalem.[90] This tradition of faith in Christ being taught by

(Hebrew) Scripture continues to assume a prominent place in Acts and becomes a model for preaching and mission: Peter at Pentecost teaches the spiritual fulfilment of Scripture, Stephen in his speech before the Council narrates allegorically the salvation history of Israel from Abraham to Christ, and Paul and Barnabas in the synagogue present Christ as the fulfilment of the Psalms.[91]

De Lubac repudiates the supposition that the Protestant Reformation brought with it a new emphasis on the place of Scripture in faith in contrast with a previous monastic preoccupation with works. He states: 'It was an almost unanimously held proposition, right up to the eve of the Reformation, that Scripture contains all of revelation.'[92] The recovery of creative and faithful scriptural reasoning in all parts of the Church remains one of the principal theological challenges for the present day.

De Lubac himself appears diffident about the contemporary usefulness of the doctrine of the fourfold sense, pointing to the dangers of its ossification and stating that theology can no longer be grounded solely in Scripture.[93] The doctrine nevertheless remains pivotal to that part of theology concerned with Scripture. De Lubac's strictures against attempting to separate historical and allegorical readings, and then supposing that the first type are more faithful to Christian faith than the second, are indeed even more pertinent now than when he articulated them. Personal conversion requires the adding together of all four senses of Scripture, which exist in a state of 'essential interdependence' and 'dynamic continuity' and can be compared to each side of a square.[94] This operation cannot be achieved by human reason unaided. The ultimate key to unlocking the truth of Scripture is Christ, who in his death and resurrection is the spirit of the letter and the head of the body of the Scriptures[95]:

> His cross is the sole and universal key. By this sacrament of the cross, he unites the two testaments into a single body of doctrine, intermingling the ancient precepts with the grace of the gospel. By dying, the Lion of Judah obtains the victory that opens the book with seven seals. He penetrates into the temple that contains the holy Ark. He rends the veil that covered the mysteries of grace.[96]

De Lubac describes Christ as the 'abridged Word' who makes possible the Christian's own effort to abridge, condense and unify

Scripture and extract its substance in truthful and comprehensible form.[97] Christ's exegesis is, therefore, not primarily words but action. As the opening of Luke's Gospel proclaims, Christ fulfils the events of which Scripture provides a written account.

CHAPTER FIVE

PERSON, WORLD AND HISTORY

De Lubac sees the whole created order of time and space as providing an analogy for human life. The human person, created in the image of a personal God, stands at the crowning point of the created order. Being the creation of God and the Spirit, the person can only be conceived in this way as existing as part of the wider created order of time and space. Yet the person, being creation's superior element, equally *contains* creation in an analogical sense: the history of the world recounted in Scripture is the progression of human life on earth, just as the ordered space of creation can be thought of as a world soul in which the spiritual, mental and material principles of the human soul are embodied. This is because time and space are also effects of divine personality. The world and its history themselves constitute God's self-revelation to humankind and the means by which God informs, redeems and transforms the human person through the work of Christ and the Spirit by raising them to new life in them. Yet because the soul *is*, analogically speaking, history and space, it also participates actively in their transformation and thus co-operates with God in its own redemption.

WRITING AND READING HISTORY

Christian history is coeval with the history of the world, beginning with the world's creation. Human history commences later with the creation of the first people to populate the world. These concrete histories are recorded in Scripture but are in essence real, lived history. God 'reveals himself in his works, manifesting to humans his unique plan of salvation, from the creation of the world up to the entry of this created world into eternal life'.[1] Scripture does not present an exhaustive, retrospective interpretation of world history, therefore, but a divinely-inspired account progressively unfolded within and as part of its human phase. De Lubac states: 'If salvation is social in its essence it follows that history is the necessary interpreter between God and humankind.'[2] This process of historical interpretation of God's revelation to humankind continues through the whole of Scripture:

> The reality which is typified in the Old – and even the New – Testament is not merely spiritual, it is incarnate; it is not merely spiritual but historical as well. For the Word was made flesh and set up his tabernacle among us. The spiritual meaning, then, is to be found on all sides, not only or more especially in a book but first and foremost *in reality itself*: 'In the very fact itself and not only in what is said about the fact we ought to seek the mystery.'[3] Indeed, what we call nowadays the Old and New Testaments is not primarily a book. It is a twofold event, a twofold 'covenant', a twofold dispensation which unfolds its development through the ages, and which is fixed, one might suppose, by no written account. When the Fathers said that God was its author – the one and only author of the Old and New Testaments – they did not liken him merely, nor indeed primarily, to a writer, but saw in him the founder, the lawgiver, the institutor of these two 'instruments' of salvation, these two economies, two dispensations.[4]

God is not so much the author of Scripture as author of the history which Scripture recounts. Scripture should therefore be regarded not as writing about history, because the writing is the history itself, but as the *reading* of history. It is in the history really written in the world by God that the exegetical and hermeneutical challenges posed by Scripture will be focused. The text is in this sense not an end in itself.

In asserting that the primary spiritual meaning of reality is exhibited within history itself, de Lubac locates scriptural interpretation inalienably in an objective, public reality. When reading specific passages, he consequently prefers images drawn from this reality rather than from the dilemmas of theoretical systematic theology or ethics. He perceives, for instance, the six ages of the world as reflected in the parables of Matthew 13.24-50, which together comprise a 'sacred history'. The sowing of bad seed signifies the corruption of God's creation due to the sins of Adam and Cain. The small mustard seed planted in the field that would grow into a tree in which birds could nest, evokes the remnant of humankind who survived the Flood and who would become the 'towering tree of all the races'. The yeast mixed with three measures of flour suggests the faith of Abraham, which spread beyond the walls of the synagogue to encompass the whole world. The treasure which is found and then hidden in the field alludes to the prophecies about Christ delivered from the time of David onwards. The pearl of great price sought by the merchant is finally discovered in the person of Christ at his birth in Bethlehem. The net thrown into the sea to catch fish of every kind is an analogy for the gathering of righteous souls into the kingdom of heaven by the angels.[5]

An especially striking instance of this allegorical reading of history is the familiar parable of the Good Samaritan. De Lubac quotes the rich allegorical exposition of this passage given by Origen, the 'man of the spirit, the apostle, the man of the church'.[6] In the parable

The man means Adam with the life he originally led and with the fall caused by disobedience. Jerusalem means paradise, or the Jerusalem on high. Jericho is the world, the robbers are the opposing powers, whether devils or false teachers, who profess to come in the name of Christ. The wounds are disobedience and sins. Man is stripped of his clothing, that is, he loses incorruptibility and immortality, he is despoiled of every virtue. He is left half dead because death has seized a half of our human nature. The priest is the law. The Levite represents the prophets. The Samaritan is Christ who took on human flesh through Mary. The beast of burden is the body of Christ.

The wine is the word of teaching and correction, the oil is the word of philanthropy, compassion or encouragement. The inn is the church. The innkeeper is the college of apostles and their successors, bishops and teachers of the churches, or else the angels who are set over the Church. The two pennies are the two Testaments, the Old and the New, or love of God and one's neighbour, or knowledge of the Father and the Son. The return from Samaria is the second coming of Christ.[7]

Some will find this comprehensive allegorization excessive. It nevertheless contrasts sharply with the modern preoccupation of moral-
izing the episode. In current readings, the man who is robbed is
typically cast as righteous rather than sinful, and as someone whose
predicament could have been resolved by benevolent human philanthropy refused by the passers-by on the road, who are sinners. The
purpose of the parable is not, however, to give an account of the way
Christians may overcome their own sinfulness by means of moral
and social self-improvement, but to speak to the whole of humanity
about its fallen condition and need of Christ. The moral reading of
the episode suggests something approaching a Jansenist account of
the relation between grace and nature, according to which good
human action compels the giving of divine grace as an external gift
to a human nature which is culturally identified as absolutely
corrupt. ('The Samaritan is the outsider, but it is he who is saved.')
In fact, only the action of Christ – the sole human action which is
good without qualification – can redeem the history of the world,
and good human action is dependent on this action and co-operates
with it. Humankind cannot, therefore, replace the work of Christ by
casting itself as the Samaritan. The human race is lying helplessly in
the dust of material life, waiting for the coming of Christ on which
history and humanity are totally dependent.

The Incarnation is chief among the successive stages of the divine
plan through which world history unfolds, being the moment at
which Christ assumes human nature.[8] It is not, crucially, a mere
image provided in order better to understand history, as in the case
of the deities of classical philosophy. In the Incarnation, Christ is
not limited by history but limits that history by enfolding and transforming it within himself and providing its ultimate end, or in Pierre
Teilhard de Chardin's phrase, its 'Omega point'.[9] Thus human
dignity is assured by the Incarnation, which exalts human greatness
and humankind's capacity to attain the end divinely offered to it.[10]
The contrast with pre-Christian thought could not be more striking:
'The idea of a spiritual reality becoming incarnate in the realm of
sense, needing time for its accomplishment, that without prejudice
to its spiritual significance should be prepared, come to pass, and
mature socially in history – such a notion is entirely alien to these
philosophers.'[11] Linear history is, in other words, a distinctively
Christian notion. The possibility of the redemption of the world by
a concrete and historic spiritual life is provided only by Christ, who

in his Incarnation assumes humankind collectively and completely into himself and spiritually transforms it. De Lubac therefore states, quoting Gregory of Nyssa: 'The whole of human nature from the first man to the last is but one image of him who is.'[12] All humanity is in this sense included in God's initial general creation of the world:

> In making a human nature, it is human nature that he united to himself, that he enclosed in himself, and it is the latter, whole and entire, that in some sort he uses as a body. He assumed in himself the nature of all flesh. Whole and entire he will raise it from the dead, whole and entire he will save it. Christ the Redeemer does not offer salvation merely to each one; he effects it, he is himself the salvation of the whole, and for each one salvation consists in a personal ratification of his original belonging to Christ, so that he be not cast out, cut off from this Whole.[13]

Reconciliation is a transformation which necessarily includes and changes the whole of the human race. Human life is lived, however, not collectively but personally, with individual lives created in the image of God. The unification of human nature in divine nature therefore establishes not only a distinctively Christian conception of corporate human nature, but also a spiritual differentiation between individually unique human persons.

THE THREEFOLD HUMANITY OF CHRIST

De Lubac challenges conceptions of human nature as inherently dualistic and oppositional, such as those which see it as bearing within itself a conflict between flesh and spirit.[14] He proposes instead a threefold model, and defends this in his essay 'Tripartite Anthropology'. A key object of this exposition is to challenge the widespread notion that the triadic model of the soul is classical (i.e. pagan) and its use by Christian theologians a distortion of true theology effected under the influence of the Platonism of Origen.[15] Models of the soul as comprising three elements, or manifesting three aspects, are certainly fundamental to the speculations of Plato. For instance, in the *Phaedrus* the three parts of the chariot – the charioteer, the black horse, and the grey – represent intellect, desire and reason.[16] Nonetheless Origen, whilst embracing a tripartite definition of the soul, explicitly rejects 'philosophical deceits' on the simple grounds that these possess no scriptural warrant.[17] A distinct threefold account of the soul can also be traced in Scripture, however. The people of Israel are commanded: 'Love the Lord your God with all your heart, and with all your soul, and with all your strength.'[18] The Psalmist praises the God in whom he takes refuge with the words 'my heart is glad, and my soul rejoices; my body also rests secure.'[19] The writer to the Thessalonians concludes his first letter by praying with the Church: 'May your spirit (*pneuma*) and soul (*psyche*) and body (*soma*) be kept sound and blameless at the coming of our Lord Jesus Christ.'[20]

These three elements should not be understood as three separate faculties but as a 'threefold zone of activity' unified in the heart.[21] Spirit, soul and body exist in a state of mutual interdependence. Soul and body rely on the spirit to provide their ultimate telos, spirit and soul depend on the body to provide them with their place in the material world, and body and spirit need the soul for the practical reasoning which binds them together. This distinction between spirit, soul and body has its roots in a major transformation of the philosophy of Aristotle. The superior element there is not spirit but *nous*, the immortal, divine principle of intellectual life, 'an independent substance implanted within us' which is 'incapable of being destroyed'. This provides a triad of mind, soul and body. The crucial Christian transition is therefore from mind into spirit.

This spiritual turn is anticipated in Jewish theology.[22] Philo of Alexandria, who flourished around the time of Christ, was imbued with the Hellenic doctrine of the contemplative *nous* but in spite of this

> does not speak of *nous* but of *pneuma*. God, he says, breathes into man a *pneuma*; not content with making him simply alive, composed of soul and body, he gave him a part of his spirit; this is what Moses teaches by saying that he made him in his image. The *pneuma*, in man, is the principle of a higher life, the place of communication with God.[23]

Philo is convinced of the necessity of the completion of soul by spirit, on which existence and salvation absolutely depend. He avers that the mind

> would be really earthly and corruptible, if it were not that God had breathed into it the spirit of genuine life; for then it 'exists',

and is no longer made into a soul; and its soul is not inactive, and incapable of proper formation, but a really intellectual and living one.[24]

The Semitic origin of the *pneuma* is evident in Philo's allusion to the second Genesis creation narrative: 'The Lord God formed man from the dust of the ground, and breathed into his nostrils the breath of life; and the man became a living being.'[25] The breathing metaphor suggests an aspect of the soul intrinsic to it rather than superadded to a pre-existing human nature, and a 'dynamic concept of humanity that excludes the notion of "pure nature" '.[26]

The activity of *pneuma* in the Jewish covenant raises the question of its newness in later explicitly Christian revelation. In John's Gospel, the breath of life is specifically associated with the Holy Spirit on the evening of the day of Christ's resurrection, when Christ appears among his gathered disciples and breathes the Spirit on them.[27] The Holy Spirit is not, in other words, just another name for the spirit of God spoken of in Hebrew Scripture. The difference is, of course, that the new *pneuma* proceeds from Christ, and is therefore the Spirit of Christ.

Discussion of the Holy Spirit has often been an embarrassment to rationalist theology.[28] De Lubac, while giving proper weight to this element of divine revelation and human anthropology, nevertheless wishes to retain an appropriate 'suspension'[29] between natural and supernatural:

> Just as it is necessary to reject an anthropology that, refusing humanity any higher faculty, stifles the spirit in it . . . so it is necessary to guard against reducing theoretical or practical reason in humanity by failing to recognize its transcendence in relation to the sensible order and its participation in the absolute.[30]

It is this suspension which establishes the unique dignity of the human person in space and time, endowing humanity with the power and responsibility to co-operate with God in transforming the world and shaping its future history. It makes every action unique and unrepeatable – in other words, it establishes a path of linear historical evolution in the Spirit towards consummation in Christ: 'Since the flow of time is irreversible nothing occurs in it more than once, so that every action takes on a special dignity and an awful gravity; and it is because the world is a history, a single history, that each individual life is a drama.'[31]

Christ reveals the likeness of God to humankind created in God's image. This image 'shines in the depths of the soul, which therefore is itself that image, yearning to be reunited with its model, it can be so only through Christ'.[32] The image of God is, however, different from his likeness, which is represented by Christ and proceeds from Christ. This theology of creation suggests, in turn, a theology of salvation grounded not in the supernatural action of Christ conceived as wholly extrinsic to human nature and independent of human initiative, but as restoring and completing the original goodness of humanity as created by God. The culmination of Christ's saving work was not his substitution of himself for humankind in bearing the weight of the sins of the world, but rather his triumph over the sinful human condition and transformation of it. Christ came into the world in order to

> enable us to raise ourselves through him to God. He came not to win for us an external pardon – that fundamentally was ours from all eternity and is presupposed by the Incarnation itself . . . but to change us inwardly. Thenceforward humanity was to cooperate actively in its own salvation, and that is why to the act of his sacrifice Christ joined the objective revelation of his person and the foundation of his Church.[33]

God calls humankind to share in his work of salvation[34] which thus becomes a process of continuous creation.[35] De Lubac is here inspired by Teilhard de Chardin's understanding of creation as a continuing transformative movement. Humankind is itself a product of the creative process, but is then called to contribute to that process in actions which intimately combine the kingdom of God with human effort, which 'co-operates in the natural fulfilment of the world'.[36]

Humanity is granted a pre-eminent place in the cosmos, combining body and intellect in productive ability and mediating material and spiritual principles. The action of God on the human person provides, moreover, an analogy for divine action in the wider created order.[37] The consequences of action are potentially unlimited and the intention motivating action transcends the immediate reality in which the action occurs. This theology of reflective action needs to be seen, more immediately, in light of de Lubac's study of Maurice Blondel, the catholic lay philosopher whose philosophy of action provided foundations for twentieth-century catholic theology. Blondel argued that any true human action implied the affirmation of a universal value. De Lubac, in his study of Pico della Mirandola, quotes Blondel's following description of humanity containing within itself the entire universe:

Man is a 'microcosm', *summa mundi et compendium* (a summation of the world and a compendium), the summary of all the experiences, of all the inventions and of all the ingenuities of nature, an extract and an original product of the whole; the universe concentrates all its rays in him. Subjective life is the substitute and the synthesis of all other phenomena whatever they may be.[38]

Thomas Aquinas similarly considers that humanity 'in a certain sense contains all things': reason which likens it to the angels, sensitive powers which it shares with animals, natural forces also possessed by plants, and the physical embodiment characteristic of matter.[39] Humanity is the true universal mediator of the world, assuring the continuity and harmony of God's creative and redemptive work.[40]

De Lubac sees Teilhard de Chardin's theory of creative transformation as anticipating his own developed notion of the supernatural. In his wartime essay 'Operative Faith' of 1917, Teilhard posits the 'integration of the natural in the supernatural':

In the material universe it is Spirit, and in Spirit it is the *moral* sphere, which are eminently the *present* centre in which life develops. It is into this flexible core of ourselves, accordingly, where grace mingles with the natural impulses of the earth, that we have forcefully to direct the power of faith. There, above all, we can count upon creative energy awaiting us, ready to transform us.[41]

The salvation of the world is equally, however, the salvation of individual human persons. Describing Teilhard's cosmology using a phrase from Irenaeus, de Lubac states: 'God made temporal things for humankind, so that coming to maturity in them it may reap the fruit of immortality.'[42]

The Word of God, states the writer to the Hebrews, penetrates to the division of soul and spirit and thus discerns the thoughts and intentions of the heart.[43] Christ's overcoming of the familiar bipolar opposition between flesh and spirit, nature and the supernatural is fundamental to de Lubac's vision: 'Spiritual unity does not include beings only in keeping them distinct, whether God and humanity, or individual human beings. It is essentially a unity of mutual love and mutual knowledge.'[44] Hence Maximus the Confessor defends Chalcedonian christology in positing the 'indivisible identity' of humanity and divinity in God in which the consummation or completion of the universe consists. There exists, from the human point of view, a certain homogeneity between God's being and manifestations: God for himself (*theos pros seaton*) is totally present in God for us (*theos pros hemas*) owing to the essentially missionary character of divine action in favour of humankind, in which God makes himself known by bringing about the salvation of humanity.[45]

De Lubac also wishes to guard against too close an identification of the Holy Spirit with the spirit of God which dwells in humankind. After all, Pelagius identifies the spirit of humankind with the Spirit of God as part of his exaltation of humanity above God. The only possible response to the contemplation of the Spirit which comes from God is 'praise and silent adoration in the recognition of the unfathomable mystery'.[46] De Lubac remains equally determined to oppose positions identified in his critique of Jansenism. These tend to the other extreme of identifying the Spirit as a gift extrinsically given to a previously sinful but now elect portion of humanity, thus granting it admission into the kingdom of God. Both the Pelagian and Jansenist extremes are in danger of ignoring the role of human initiative and response to the Spirit of God. For Pelagius, relationality is effectively abolished, while with Jansenius it is unclear how the person, before receiving the Spirit, is able to make any kind of preparation for it or response to it, while after the time of receiving, humanity seems to be necessarily under grace.

De Lubac negotiates these twin hazards by describing the Holy Spirit as the 'spirit of the man which is in him':

The *pneuma* that is 'in man', in every man, assures a certain hidden transcendence of the man over himself, a certain opening, a certain received continuity between man and God. Not that there is the least identity of essence between the one and the other . . . but it is, at the heart of man, the privileged place, always intact, of their encounter.[47]

Pneuma is divine life in itself, but also divine life shared with humanity: 'the creature itself becomes *pneuma*, in the measure that it possesses this life.' To use a Neoplatonic analogy, humankind participates in divine life to a degree apposite to its level of perfection in the scale of being:

> The Spirit of God, even when it is present in us, is one thing, and the *pneuma* proper to every man, that which is in him, is something else . . . The Apostle clearly affirms that this spirit (this *pneuma*) is different from the Spirit of God, even when the Holy Spirit is present in us, over and above the spirit of man that is in him.[48]

The *pneuma* is not part of human personality, and cannot therefore be manifested directly to the world by verbal testimony, smiling, other physical actions, nor any other practical means.

In this union the distinctiveness of divine and human elements is maintained. It is by no means an admixture of divine and human properties. Teilhard de Chardin's axiom that 'union differentiates' is instructive here, having the status of both a law of being and an ethical principle law. De Lubac refers to the 'gulf which persists even in union – that separates the natural from the supernatural', and continues, 'Nature is, as it were, "matter" offered to the supernatural.'[49] He here evokes the opening words of Teilhard's striking meditation 'The Priest': 'Since today, Lord, I your Priest have neither bread nor wine nor altar, I shall spread my hands over the whole universe and take its immensity as the matter of my sacrifice.'[50] Teilhard introduces his 'Mass on the World' with a similar statement: 'Since once again, Lord . . . I have neither bread, nor wine, nor water, I will raise myself beyond these symbols, up to the pure majesty of the real itself; I, your priest, will make the whole earth my altar and on it will offer you all the labours and sufferings of the world.'[51] De Lubac offers the following synopsis of Teilhard's thesis: 'It is the nature of lower things to be drawn to and absorbed in the higher, not in such a way that they cease to be, but so that they are more fully preserved in the higher, and they subsist, and are one.'[52]

Just as illuminating is de Lubac's discussion of Pico della Mirandola's treatise *On Being and the One*. The Italian Renaissance

Neoplatonist here refutes two concepts of God's relation to the created order: that God is no more than *ens* (being in the world), and that God is beyond *esse* (being in itself). De Lubac identifies the first position, which amounts to pantheism, with Averroës and certain Thomists in the analytical tradition, and the second with Proclus.[53] Pico does not suppose that the unity of being and the One has already been fully achieved, distinguishing clearly between unity *in* God, which God possesses for himself, and unity *after* God, which other things receive from God. He states: 'In the being of things, we can admire the power of God working . . . who united each thing to itself, then all things to each other, then all things to himself, calling each thing to love of itself, of other things, and finally of God.'[54] In the *Heptaplus*, Pico presents the negative aspect of this theology. Discord is everywhere, he accepts, although never in pure or complete form: even disunity contains the promise of unification and redemption. Humankind is confronted with 'discordant concord', which for Pico as for de Lubac can only be resolved in Christ, who is truth itself, and a principle of synthesis because the bond of the whole created order.[55] In the words of the writer to the Colossians, Christ is 'before all things, and in him all things hold together'.[56]

Faith in Christ is a spiritual encounter, indeed *the* encounter.[57] De Lubac for this reason attaches great significance to Christ's naming of the apostles when he calls them. Indeed, his naming of the apostles actually constitutes his call to them. Christ calls the Christian by a new name which expresses God's personal relationship to every Christian, written in the book of life and acknowledged by Christ before the Father. The model for the Christian's response to this call is provided by the example of Christ himself:

> In Jesus Christ, the perfect meeting of God and man, both call and response, revelation and faith are united; in him is perfectly expressed, in a unique Amen, the twofold 'Yes' of God to man and of man to God; the marriage between the Creator and his creation is consummated. In each of those who believe in him, in proportion to his faith, this marvel is renewed.[58]

Christ therefore both announces God's call to humanity and exemplifies the faithful response to it, providing the model for obedient discipleship as well as its very possibility. The Christian community is called to model itself on this same personal, relational life such that it becomes the 'place par excellence of personal relationships'.[59] This personal mode of living will govern the Christian community's mission and the ways in which it shows Christ to others. De Lubac states:

> The mystery of the Trinity was not made known to us as a sublime theory, a celestial theorem, with no connection with what we are and what we must become. God, the creator of our world, has chosen to intervene in our history. It is by acting in our favour, by calling us to himself, by bringing about our salvation, that he has made himself known to us.[60]

Encounter suggests a reciprocity between the human person and God. Initiative nevertheless rests wholly with God, whose revelation is itself personalizing. Humanity, in response to God's call, discovers and acknowledges God as the personal Absolute. Encounter is therefore given the name 'revelation' when considered from God's perspective.[61] The Godhead exemplifies an intensified form of personality, which de Lubac describes at one point as 'tripersonality'.[62] In so doing he does not wish to posit any division within the divine unity, but rather to demonstrate how the perfect mutuality in which the unity of divine personality consists is the source of the unity of human personality.

De Lubac criticizes the displacement of the personal soul in theological discourse by the notion of subjectivity. Theologians sometimes appear willing to begin their reflections with an unreconstructed notion of 'the self' and its needs and desires that is more reliant on sociological and psychological theories than on a theological understanding of the soul formed, informed and preserved in its encounter with Christ. Such approaches are often defended on the grounds that they bring theology into dialogue with secular disciplines and make it relevant to 'real life'. In fact they more often replace distinctively Christian notions like knowledge of the heart, interior illumination and spiritual communion with the phantasm of a model of the soul that is purely natural.[63] They thereby contribute to the formation of an administrative, rationalized and totalizing universe of which a principal spatial manifestation is soulless, depersonalized urbanization. De Lubac sees so many modern humans '*absent* from each other . . . because they are absent from themselves, since they have abandoned this Eternal which alone establishes them in being and enables them to communicate with one another'.[64]

The tendency to employ the resulting modern, autonomous, atomized conceptions of humanity as a model for God needs to be resisted. Such models have become virtually normative in large sectors of systematic theology, being afforded more credence than they merit because their notions of divine authority, power and initiative are in superficial continuity with the classic concept of God as the omnipotent source of all being. In fact, personality is frequently replaced by *subjectivity* in the model of the Godhead developed.[65] Karl Barth – who introduced de Lubac to shark-fin soup at a Chinese restaurant in Paris – is for this reason prevented, de Lubac argues, from giving a 'proper consistency to the human spirit considered in its relation to God'.[66] Barth insists that *pneuma* is not a property of humanity but a gratuitous gift which at death must be returned to God and which persists, and which God either withdraws from humanity or grants to humanity. Barth defines the 'differentiating exaltation and distinction of man' as the 'fact that he is not just earth moulded into a body, and not just a soul, but a soul quickened and established and sustained by God in a direct and personal and special encounter of His breath with this frame of dust'. Barth nevertheless resists absolutely the notion that the human soul is 'trichotomous'. The Spirit, he argues, binds body and soul together not as a third aspect of humanity but as the 'divine address and gift to man'.[67] The view that the spirit was also part of the soul would necessarily issue, Barth argues, in the concept of two distinct souls and the rupture of humanity's being.[68] De Lubac certainly wishes to retain an appropriate bipartite tension between the Spirit of God in himself and the spirit of God in humanity, but situates this within a tripartite and Trinitarian conception of the human person.

GOD, PERSON AND WORLD

De Lubac regards self-knowledge and self-respect as the foundations of socially and politically responsible action in the world. The divine principle is itself defined by Aristotle as thought thinking itself, which suggests that reflection possesses an intrinsically spiritual quality which allows a degree of participation by God in humanity's being.[69] De Lubac interprets the Delphic command 'Know thyself!' in Christian terms as 'Learn how to see in yourself the spirit, which is a reflection of God, made for God.'[70] The person, he believes, acquires dignity not by means of egoistic self-assertion in opposition to the rest of humanity, but by self-reflection through which they see their being and final end as given by God.

The Delphic commandment is politically and theologically relevant, de Lubac argues, because humanity is a microcosm within which is contained the whole universe.[71] Gregory of Nyssa therefore fuses Delphic and Christian concerns when interpreting the advice of the bridegroom's friends in the opening chapter of the Song of Songs:

> 'If you do not know yourself, beautiful one among women, go in the footsteps of the flocks and feed your kids by the shepherds' tents.' What does this mean? The person ignorant of himself leaves the flocks of sheep and feeds with the goats whom Christ has rejected at his left hand.[72]

The soul's departure from religious truth is due, in this passage, to its lack of self-knowledge. De Lubac transposes this patristic insight into an entirely new political setting. Certain modern interpretations of the reciprocal relation between the soul (or person) and world, including Schopenhauer's, suggest that the soul, by accepting its place in the world, surrenders its capacity for spontaneous action. De Lubac believes in contrast that the reciprocal relation between soul and world in fact abolishes the ideologies of fate or destiny on which political oppression so often depends, arguing that the world is in fact dependent for its freedom on the action of the person whose conscience is informed by God. He is determined above all to refute the view that political events are preordained, retaining faith in the capacity of humanity for reason and dialogue: war between nations, for instance, is not inevitable, whatever the realist model of international politics might assert.

Many pastoral theologians currently emphasize the value of an awareness of human vulnerability in Christian life and ministry for providing the essential basis for human transformation. De Lubac proposes the opposite, affirming the historic Christian tradition of the greatness and potential glory of humanity because created in the image of God and transformed into God's likeness. In *The Drama of Atheist Humanism*, he cites Clement of Alexandria:

> Hail, O light! For in us, buried in darkness, shut up in the shadow of death, light has shone forth from heaven, purer than the sun,

sweeter than life here below. That light is eternal life; and whatever partakes of it lives . . . For 'the Sun of Righteousness' . . . has raised us to the skies, transplanting mortality into immortality, and translating earth to heaven . . . deifying us by heavenly teaching, putting His laws into our minds, and writing them on our hearts . . . The heavenly and truly divine love comes to us thus, when in the soul itself the spark of true goodness, kindled in the soul by the Divine Word, is able to burst forth into flame; and, what is of the highest importance, salvation runs parallel with sincere willingness – choice and life being, so to speak, yoked together.[73]

Clement here suggests a close connection between personal self-esteem and respect for God, and that as one increases so does the other. De Lubac implies, furthermore, that the more the soul respects God *and itself* the more likely it is to be struck by the divine image in other human souls.

Christian religion has, unfortunately, frequently departed from the humanism of Clement by seeking to separate these two forms of respect, and has become at times an enemy of human dignity. In the context of spiritual guidance, the sacrament of reconciliation or ministerial formation, to take three instances, excessive personal criticism by well-intentioned but misguided mentors might lead to a decline in a person's self-esteem, and as a corollary, to a decline in their respect for the dignity of others around them or even to a diminished sense of Christian vocation. De Lubac applies a similar insight on a global scale, supporting Proudhon's argument that modern humanism – which includes both Nazism and communism – is constructed on foundations provided by modern society's resentment of the denial of human dignity by a substantial strand of misguided Christian teaching. This is why de Lubac often employs the term 'antitheism' rather than 'atheism': the ideologies of modern humanism remain parasitic on the belief they purport to deny.[74] De Lubac says of the antitheism which Christianity has spawned:

At its maximum point of concentration, it is the great crisis of modern times, that same crisis in which we are involved today and which takes its outward course in disorder, begets tyrannies and collective crimes, and finds its expression in blood, fire and ruin.[75]

De Lubac describes Nietzsche's prediction of the advent of nihilism as being the 'effect, the manifestation of a deeper and a purely inward crisis'. Nihilism as a social phenomenon is founded on a loss of self-confidence by individual human persons, the origins of which lie ultimately in distorted forms of Christian practice. Nietzsche, de Lubac reminds us, has positive things to say about primitive Christianity in his early works, commending the way in which its Dionysian spirit usurped 'effeminate Greece', as well as its exaltation of martyr-saints.[76] De Lubac, while not of course promoting the full excesses of the Dionysian spirit, states that 'in the present state of the world Christianity *must* become a heroic Christianity,' which includes the 'courage to call evil by its proper name'. He says of this renewed form of Christian witness: 'It will consist, *above all*, in resisting with courage, in face of the world and perhaps against one's own self, the lures and seductions of a false ideal, and in proudly maintaining, in their paradoxical intransigence, the Christian values that are threatened and derided.'[77]

De Lubac argues convincingly that Nietzsche's protest is not, in fact, against Christian faith per se, but against the Christianity of his own time, asking rhetorically: 'His cutting scorn is aimed at our mediocrities and hypocrisies; he aims at our weaknesses embellished with fine names. Can we blame him completely? Must everything that "bears the name of Christian today" be defended against him?'[78] The correct response is not reversion to forms of Christian living buttressed by the privileges of wealth and political power, but 'returning to Christianity its power in us; which means, above all, of rediscovering it such as it is in itself, in its purity and in its authenticity . . . There is nothing to be changed, nothing to be added; it does not need to be adapted to the fashion of the day. We must return it to itself in our souls. We must return our souls to it.'[79] In his study of Pico della Mirandola, de Lubac observes that the Renaissance celebration of human dignity, far from being novel or a threat to Christian witness, recapitulates the synthesizing efforts of early Christian thinkers like Gregory of Nyssa and Maximus the Confessor. The humanism of Pico's *Oratio* celebrates Adam and Christ just as much as Prometheus, and provides the modern roots for an authentic Christian humanism.[80]

CHAPTER SIX

FAITH, BELIEF AND REASON

In 1961 de Lubac wrote the preface to a collection of writings by the poet Paul Claudel. He quotes in his text Claudel's dramatic description of his response to hearing the chanted words of the Creed:

> It seems to me that I am witnessing the creation of the world. I know how much they have cost – each of its expressions, each of those printed statements of eternal truth. I know what convulsions, what wrenchings of heaven and earth, what torrents of blood, what efforts, what parturition of the intelligence and what effusions of grace were required for their emergence. I see those great dogmatic continents, one after the other, rise up, and take shape before my eyes, and I see humanity in labour, finally succeeding in tearing from its heart the definitive expression.[1]

This arresting imagery outlines some of the questions to be explored in this chapter. De Lubac refuses simple oppositions between reason and faith, private belief and public belief, theology and action. The Creeds are so important to him because they express in conceptual, public terms the essential content of faith to which the Church progressively gave birth in the earliest centuries of its life. Nevertheless, the act of faith, in other words the simple act of believing in God, is not provided by credal affirmation, but arises prior to it. Therefore the '*objective* language of the Creed must be the manifestation of the *existential* language of the act to which it testifies'.[2] The definitions of belief contained in the Creed are products of human reason, yet describe a transcendent reality. They cannot, as such, be of purely natural origin. Belief is not simply knowledge *about* God, but knowledge *of* God in which God actively reveals himself. Belief is therefore dependent on God for its specific content as well as its original possibility.

FAITH AND THE IDEA OF GOD

In 1910 the Jesuit theologian Pierre Rousselot published an article titled 'The Eyes of Faith' in the new journal *Recherches de science religieuse*.[3] Rousselot had suggested that participation in church practices and other outward forms of assent to Christian truth needed to be accompanied by a distinct 'psychological' assent. This can be thought of as an act of the inner person rather than a public observance, and was termed by Rousselot an 'act of faith'. Scholastic theologians including Hippolyte Ligeard and Stéphane Harent strongly opposed his thesis, defending the standard opinion that church teaching should command the immediate assent of believers simply by virtue of its status as the teaching of the Church. They considered the suggestion that a distinct 'act of faith' was needed as part of the assent to Christian truth to be false and subversive, even though there was no suggestion that an inward assent of faith would undermine existing teaching. Rousselot was killed fighting with the French army at Éparges in 1915, but his doctrine lived on and gained increasing numbers of adherents. The necessity of personal assent to doctrine, and more importantly to the person of God, is now axiomatic in mainstream Christian theology. Nevertheless, as recently as 1920 the 'act of faith' theology had been banned within the Society of Jesus in a ruling binding on all its members, including de Lubac, following an assessment conducted by an international committee of theologians at the request of the Superior General, Wlodimir Ledochowski.[4]

Not long after the prohibition, de Lubac began circumspectly questioning the official position on the act of faith in his early articles interrogating the concept of pure nature. He wished to promote, in contrast, the view that a continuity existed from grace to nature, constituted by the natural desire for God implanted in the human soul at its creation. Indeed, de Lubac's concept of *désir naturel* already discussed provided the basis for an account of why an act of faith by the human person was possible. These notions originate in de Lubac's historical study of the Augustinian tradition begun not long after the 1920 prohibition, during his theological training at the Jesuit scholasticate in exile at Ore Place, Hastings.[5] Personal affirmative faith remained a guiding principle in his theology. In 1969 he described the act of faith as the 'fundamental attitude which makes one a Christian, the spiritual reality which lies at the root of all Christian life'.[6]

De Lubac argues that the idea of God is naturally present to the human mind prior to any explicit reasoning or objective conceptualization.[7] He describes this natural presence as a 'habit of God' in the mind[8] that is unique among concepts in not arising from any prior chain of reasoning. It cannot be fitted into any system, and is neither an axiom, nor a deduction of discursive reason. De Lubac praises Tertullian's description of the 'witness of the naturally Christian soul' grounded in the 'divine image that every person has within them and that gropingly searches for the only religion capable of uniting it with its model'.[9] As the first Latin Father states: 'O noble testimony of the soul by nature Christian! . . . It looks not to the Capitol, but to the heavens. It knows that there is the throne of the living God, as from him and from thence itself came down.'[10] This encomium on the soul is echoed in de Lubac's more philosophical identification of an 'original assent springing from being itself, which the entire role of my free will is to ratify, whatever the cost'.[11]

The idea of God is a 'reality: the very soul of the soul; a spiritual image of the Divinity, an "eikon"'.[12] De Lubac considers the affirmation that God exists to be implicit in the human soul's affirmation of its own existence. The soul possesses

> a certain 'habitual knowledge' of itself, real in spite of being obscure and veiled, constant although forever fleeting – owing to the fact that it is always present to itself; the presence of the soul present to itself, in which it may learn, as in a mirror, the presence of God to the soul. In the same way that the reality of the divine image in the soul is at the centre and principle of all rational activity, which should lead it from knowledge of the world to the affirmation of God, so, in the same way, the soul's habitual knowledge of itself can become the principle of an intimate process of reflection, enabling it to recognize its reality as 'image'.[13]

The idea of God emerges spontaneously as part of a reflective process which includes both rational and mystical elements, and imposes itself on the human mind through its own necessity.[14] De

Lubac describes the birth of the idea of God in the mind using many different terms: encounter, contact, apperception, illumination of intellect, vision, hearing, faith. He is not concerned to offer a single definitive account of this birth, but to establish certain principles which any particular account would need to satisfy.

A classic objection to this type of reciprocal definition of God's relation to humanity and humanity's relation to God is that the concept of God which emerges is dependent on cultural notions of human nature, rather than being established independently of them and thus being able to interrogate them. De Lubac was certainly aware of the ways in which the critiques of nineteenth-century religious sceptics like Feuerbach, Marx and Nietzsche were heavily reliant for their success on particular anti-humanistic notions of religion, and how they presented the Christian faith specifically as a phantasm of the human imagination. One way of reading de Lubac's argument is as a response to these and other theorists of suspicion advanced by appropriating their own methodology. More fundamentally however, de Lubac intuits that it is impossible to separate the idea of God from humanity's idea of itself. 'Absolute' knowledge would, in denying the intrinsically relational character of knowledge, 'automatically involve the disappearance of the person who is to have it'.[15] Even theologians who maintain a strong sense of the simplicity and omnipotence of God often seem, on closer examination, to be presenting an image of God based on modern individualist and subjectivist notions of *humanity* by regarding divinity as an autonomous source of power, initiative and decision.

This is not, however, to present a critique of dialectical theology and its strong conviction of the impossibility of any relational mediation between God and humanity. It is simply to suggest that theologians err when they fail to accept that the idea of God is dependent on human consciousness. An idea of God which its proponents claim to be wholly objective and entirely independent of human consciousness will quite possibly have concealed within it particular suppositions which present God in the image of particular powerful voices in Church or theology and silence other voices. The idea of God is not, however, purely subjective, being grounded in the core reality of human being given by God in creation. The idea 'God' is, in a sense, simultaneously both objective and subjective, or expressed more precisely, grounded in an intersubjectivity between God and the human soul in which God is no longer thought as an external *He* but as *Thou*, a 'subject to whom one gives oneself' and 'in whom one finds oneself'.[16] The soul encounters in the reality of God the idea of God already subsisting in its understanding. De Lubac remarks: 'The extraordinary thing is that in knowing God for the first time I do, in fact, recognize him.'[17]

BELIEF IN GOD

Christians often affirm that they 'believe in God' without fully considering what they mean. Agnostics and atheists are also happy to affirm that they 'do not believe in God'. This latter statement refusing belief appears grammatically as a negation of the first. Its meaning is, in fact, very different.

In his discussion of the Apostles' Creed, de Lubac considers at length the meaning of belief *in* God. There are very few cases in which people state a belief *in* something and mean the same thing as in this one. I might say that 'I believe in a particular trusted friend,' but then I am doing something like affirming my confidence that they will act in a trustworthy manner or carry through a project to completion. I might make a similar statement about God, which would amount to an expression of trust in divine providence. I might say alternatively that 'I believe in fairies.' This statement has a meaning apparently closer to what I would usually intend when affirming 'I believe in God,' because both involve a claim about existence versus non-existence. This similarity of meaning is, however, superficial. The statement 'I believe in fairies' is an existence claim based possibly on evidence of sorts, but probably on no more than whimsical guesswork. It is hard to think of ways in which human life would be significantly different if fairies existed from how it would be if they did not. It is equally difficult to think of ways in which our assurance of the existence of fairies would affect the nature of our belief about them. 'I believe in God' is, in contrast, more than a statement of trust and more than an existence claim, because it implies a relation between the believer and the object in whom the believer places their belief. De Lubac draws the following distinction between three kinds of belief *in*: 'The very infidels can believe that God exists (*Deum esse*); they may even believe things about God (*credere Deo*), and yet not have true faith, or at least complete faith, because they do not believe in God (*in Deum*).'[18] Even the demons believe things about God, and shudder.[19] Augustine urges

that you should believe in him; not that you should believe
things about him. But if you believe in him, that is because you
believe what you have heard about him; whereas whoever
believes things about him does not by that fact believe in him;
for the demons too believe truths about him but still do not
believe in him.[20]

Relationality and personal recognition are, in other words, intrinsic
to belief in God:

> Only that being which is at once personal and transcendent, only
> the one who is the Absolute, and the absolutely personal, the
> source and locus of all spirits, is worthy to receive the homage of
> our faith. So, we do not believe generally *in aliquem*, in someone,
> any person whatever, but *in solum Deum*, in God alone . . . To
> believe, in the full sense of the word as we have defined it from our
> consideration of the Creed, i.e., to believe absolutely, uncondi-
> tionally, definitively, in a way that irrevocably involves the very
> depths of our being, to believe with that kind of faith is not pos-
> sible unless we believe in that personal, unique Being whom we
> call God.[21]

When reciting the Apostles' Creed, I do not however say 'I believe in
the Church.' My statements of belief *in* are confined to the Father,
Son and Holy Spirit of the Godhead. They imply a 'revelation of
God concerning himself – culminating in Christ' and suggest a 'corresponding attitude of soul'.[22] Belief in God 'implies a search, an
advance, a movement of the soul (*credendo in Deum ire*); it implies a
personal impulse and, last, an adherence, which cannot find the term
of their action in anything created.'[23]

Faith is God's testimony and 'does not remain, like human testimony, entirely extrinsic to the mind that receives it'. God is not exterior to the beings he has created and who believe in him. God is, in
contrast, 'wholly other than the other', and divine transcendence
brings with it – indeed makes possible – an intimate presence: 'The
voice resounds both outside and inside of the one God calls to
believe, and it is in this sense that one can say that the experience of
God, which is a sacred experience, since it is the experience of the
sacrosanct, is not a simple experience of otherness.'[24] Faith is the
response to the call of God, an act not of knowledge about God but

one of recognition of God, who also has faith. De Lubac explains: 'When I believe *in* God, when I give him my faith, when in answer to his initiative I turn myself over to him from the bottom of my being, there is established between him and me a bond of reciprocity of such a kind that the same word, faith, can be applied to each of the two partners.'[25] The collective belief of the Church emerges from this personal relational belief in God, which itself provides the possibility of the mutual recognition of faith.

ARGUING FOR GOD

This personal, relational affirmation of faith does not remain self-sufficient. Human beings are reasoning beings, and if faith is to be an affirmation of the whole person then it is partly a rational affirmation. A reflective moment is bound to arise sooner or later, and is indeed never entirely absent. It is experienced as a step back from the immediacy of faith: 'Reflection implies a pause, detachment, severance; initially, at any rate, a sort of question mark.'[26] This might be the result of a questioning of some aspect of tradition or a response to some perception of error or revolt which stimulates an instinctual intellectual reaction in the person of faith.

The most basic form of reasoning about faith is arguing for God's existence. Such arguments are implicit in many forms of theological discourse. The so-called 'proofs' for God's existence have featured prominently in classical philosophical theology in their ontological, cosmological, teleological and moral forms. De Lubac, while affirming the personal character of faith, mounts a trenchant defence of the validity of the proofs for God's existence:

> All the objections brought against the various proofs of the existence of God are in vain; criticism can never invalidate them, for it can never get its teeth into the principle common to them all. On the contrary, that principle emerges more clearly as the elements with which the proofs are constructed are rearranged. That is because it is not a particular principle which the mind can either isolate and sift so as to determine its limits, or reject out of hand: it forms part of the substance of the mind.[27]

Ideas about God motivate and sustain faith in God. They are, as has already been shown, part of a movement of the soul inspired by God and directed toward God. The intellect which apprehends God recognizes the internal dynamism by which it is illuminated. The affirmation of God must objectify itself, de Lubac argues, in order to become a 'judgment among other judgments'.[28] If the idea of God is to acquire meaning and significance in concrete life by informing rational processes and ethical decisions, then this idea needs to be articulated.

The conceptual articulation of divine reality is motivated by a fundamental human need to understand reality. Human reason is not satisfied with knowing an effect without knowing its cause, remaining in a state of continuous movement, disquiet and unrest that 'lasts until reason, moving from effect to effect and from cause to cause, at last reaches the supreme cause from which everything derives, and which, by that very fact, explains and so unifies everything'.[29] The idea of God is, as already discussed, present in the human mind from its beginning, prior to conceptual knowledge and arguments. It nevertheless is unable, having grasped the mind, to be grasped by the mind without the assistance of concepts and argument. This does not mean that the idea of God becomes objectified by rational processes. The function of the proofs for God's existence is essentially to clear away obstacles to a clearer perception of divine reality: the proofs are *ways*, and not foundations of a system of knowledge.[30] The idea of God is not, therefore, dependent on the proofs. Rather, the proofs are dependent on the idea, which provides the 'inspiration, the motive power and the justification of them all'.[31]

Human knowledge of God is real knowledge, despite being obscure, veiled and latent, and needs to be recollected by a process of continuing ratification:

> If we consider the affirmation of God where alone it exists in act, where alone it is really made, in the concrete intelligence which is at the same time a particular subject, in the responsible person that is, then the affirmation of God can be seen to be an act which is unlike any other. There is something of it in the ontological argument, and something of it in the wager; though it is neither the one nor the other. It expresses the most luminous evidence and attests the most obscure truth. Of all our acts, it is the most free and the most necessary. It is the most enduring of affirmations and the most personal of all engagements.[32]

This association of the knowledge of God with concrete life and personal responsibility reminds us that its pursuit is habitual and not an activity of a purely purposive, conscious type. The primary challenge in religious epistemology is, therefore, to cultivate the right dispositions to enable the soul to encounter God without it needing to search for God intentionally.[33] In learning with God, the most significant outcomes are often the unintended ones.

Much disputation about Christian faith takes place in the context of doubt about God's existence, character or providence. Anselm's ontological argument and Pascal's wager both referred to above are two examples of reasoning about the possibility that God does not exist, but each concludes on different grounds that God cannot *not* exist. De Lubac's sympathy for Pascal's wager might seem quixotic. The wager is frequently presented as a cynical hedging of bets motivated by an awareness that the future consequences for an individual of not believing in God then discovering that God exists are worse than those of believing in God then discovering that God does not exist. De Lubac rightly understands Pascal's faith in more profound terms than these. The wager is in fact motivated by emotion, and more specifically by fear of the 'eternal silence' of the 'infinite spaces' generated by seventeenth-century scientific advances.[34] The distress and anguish experienced in the face of the dislocation they brought motivate an affirmation of God's existence.[35] It is not the possible future consequences of denying that God exists which motivate assent to the proposition that God does exist. Rather the current intellectual and emotional consequences of such a denial lead Pascal beyond the absurdity of denial, in faith, to profession. The dynamic of this movement is not calculating assent but the illumination of the mind by God.

Recognition of a principle transcending nature is, de Lubac states, essential to human life, giving to human nature its purpose and meaning: 'Humans are of absolute value, because they are illuminated by a ray of light from the face of God; because, although they develop as they act in history, they breathe the air of eternity.'[36] Failure to recognize the dependence of humanity on God reduces the whole of life to duration: a state of unceasing change with no guiding principle. The affirmation of the existence of an Absolute is essential for human flourishing. De Lubac identifies various instances in his writings of people whose dignity is destroyed by their refusal to make such an affirmation. One example is Friedrich

Nietzsche, who 'killed himself, his mind foundered in perpetual night, because he proclaimed, accepted and willed "the death of God" '.[37] Nietzsche refused to accept that humanity 'needs a beyond which can never be grasped . . . a movement towards transcendence at the very heart of immanence . . . an eschatological beyond, already present and active in the womb of becoming'.[38]

De Lubac's discussion of Teilhard de Chardin's proof for God's existence provides some further insights into the relation between observation and illumination in thinking about God. Teilhard's argument for God's existence is cosmological. He perceives, by means of scientific observation, that the world is going through a process of convergent evolution, the sufficient reason and cause of which is the action of a unifying being.[39] De Lubac states of Teilhard:

> He knows, in fact, that the reality of Christ can in no manner be *deduced* from the World, but he also knows that revelation consolidates, extends, achieves the work sketched by reason. He discovers with joy a 'remarkable similarity' between the dogmatic perspectives and the conclusions or the ultimate hypotheses to which the study of the phenomenon of man leads him, a similarity that he attributes with good reason to the 'influence' and the 'radiation' of Christian revelation. Between reason and faith, as between nature and grace, if there is discontinuity, distinction and hierarchy, there is also just as much harmony.[40]

De Lubac accepts that Teilhard sometimes places excessive emphasis on harmony and too little on paradox. Nevertheless, Teilhard's belief in the scientific character of his proofs and their foundation in observation of the world suggests that reason is both dependent on revelation and prepares the mind to receive revelation. Reason and revelation both have roles in Teilhard's theological cosmology, providing a vision of the world sustained by divine activity and given its final goal by God. A further significant point is that Teilhard's cosmology is profoundly anthropological and personalistic.[41] God, in creating humans as material, conscious and spiritual beings, and therefore personal beings, is necessarily a personal God. It is, in turn, because of the reflective capacity which is part of the essence of human personality that humanity becomes aware of God's existence and action on the world. De Lubac cites the following statement of

Teilhard's to describe the transition from purely rational acknowledgement into personal encounter: 'When thought has reached that peak of intensity it must succeed, somehow, as a result of hyper-centration, in breaking through the temporo-spatial membrane of the phenomenon – until it joins up with a supremely personal, supremely personalizing, being.'[42]

De Lubac does not, however, advocate an inevitable confession of faith that denies the real possibility of doubt in the face of apparently contradictory evidence. Although faith is a movement of affirmation in opposition to denial, it does not refuse the option of that denial. Yet there always persists the possibility of faith beyond doubt. De Lubac states: 'Whenever we say "No", we imply that on a deeper level there is a "Yes" which provokes and originates it; rebellion always implies an acquiescence which is both deeper and more free.'[43] Doubt and struggle are, he suggests, part of any real faith, but the prior call to affirmation means that the denial of God's existence and moral character are ultimately unable to provide the human soul with the dignity it seeks in making that denial.

De Lubac is convinced that the power of affirmation is greater than that of conception or argument, reviving these and enabling them to attain a conclusion.[44] His belief in the supremacy of the affirmative mode over the negative is inspired by the philosophy of Maurice Blondel, who argues that in any human act, however apparently insignificant it may be, an objective affirmation is always and inevitably present.[45] The assertion of any particular truth is justified, Blondel argues, when it becomes part of an affirmation of universal truth.[46] The French university philosophy of Blondel's day was caustically secular, and his argument therefore an audacious attempt to challenge some of its most fundamental axioms by breaking out of purely philosophical boundaries by means of philosophy itself. De Lubac describes the likely effects of Blondel's work on an analytic philosopher: 'Shaking him out of a *critical slumber*, which, without being any better, has too often replaced the old dogmatic slumber, it will plunge him into full reality, snatch him from artificial problems and force him to see the problem as a whole.'[47] The mystery of God thus comes to penetrate reason, and not the reverse.[48] As Maximus the Confessor states:

In no way can the soul attain the knowledge of God, unless God himself stoops down to her, in order to raise her up to himself. For the human spirit would never have the strength to stay the course, so as to attain some measure of divine light, if God did not draw it to himself – inasmuch as it is possible for the human spirit to be thus drawn – and illuminate it with his own brightness.[49]

Human affirmation of God's existence and knowledge of God's being are signs of the illuminating presence and activity of God in humanity.[50] De Lubac presents theology and faith as intimately related: the reasoning about God in which the theologian engages is not a poor substitute for the practical business of church ministry, but a striking sign of divine illumination sustaining individual quests for understanding as well as the collective growth of the whole Church into deeper spiritual truth.

De Lubac's study of Anselm of Canterbury's conception of faith is particularly illuminating. De Lubac does not portray Anselm's onto-logical argument as arriving at a clear and complete demonstration of God's existence. Rather 'Anselm recognizes that even in his illumina-tion he remains in the shadows; and from these shadows, more deeply conscious of them even than at his point of departure, offers up a more anguished call of desire.'[51] As de Lubac states elsewhere, nature appears 'foreign' and 'bruised' when carried towards the super-natural.[52] He reads beyond the pivotal sixteenth chapter of the *Proslogion*, at which point the affirmative (cataphatic) description of God characteristic of the first two thirds of the book is confronted with the negative (apophatic) language expressing divine ineffability dominant in the remainder: 'How far you are from me who am so close to you! How distant you are from my sight while I am so present to your sight! You are wholly present everywhere and I do not see you. In you I move and in you I have my being and I cannot come near to you. You are within me and around me and I do not have any experi-ence of you.'[53] The pathos, sadness and melancholy in Anselm's med-itation forms part of a quasi-existential knowledge of God which resonates with much twentieth-century writing. Feeling and emotion are thus tremendously significant in the quest for knowledge of God.

In the course of his discussion of Anselm, de Lubac raises an important point about the nature of Anselm's similarity with Aquinas. Theologians often argue that Anselm portrays a more col-laborative 'Augustinian' relation between reason and faith than Aquinas. The view that Aquinas clearly separates reason from faith has, however, recently been challenged by an array of writers who, wishing to demonstrate their Thomist credentials in a new age, have tended to present the traditional 'Anselmian' view of the relation as exemplifying Aquinas's own. De Lubac reverses this association, however, suggesting that Anselm's understanding of the relation between reason and revelation is more like the one classically and correctly attributed to Aquinas,[54] namely that reason and revelation are opposed. De Lubac accepts that, according to Anselm, both mystical and rational forms of intelligence desire knowledge of God and proceed from faith. Reason and faith are nevertheless opposed to one other in their methods and expectations, existing in a direct relation of unending tension, contradiction and dialectic.[55] The apophatic moment generated by this relation is a consequence of the nature of the knowledge being sought. De Lubac states:

> Whatever is understood through knowledge is delimited by the understanding of the one who knows. So, if you have understood, it is not God. If you are able to understand, it is because you mistook something else for God. If you almost understood, it is again because you allowed your own thoughts to deceive you.[56]

Darkness, shadows and silence are therefore valuable moments in the search for God in an ongoing movement between affirmation and denial.[57] God is revealed in absence, announcing himself as 'I am he who is,' as well as in personality, disclosing himself as 'I am who I am.'[58]

CHRISTIAN PHILOSOPHY?

One way in which faith progresses towards fuller affirmation of God is by differentiating revelation, whose discourse is theology, from reason, which employs philosophy. 'The work of St Thomas Aquinas', de Lubac avers, 'marked progress of the first rank in the history of the human mind when it established, within the heart of Christian thought, the permanent distinction between philosophy and theology.'[59] De Lubac insists that although reason reveals an inferior degree of truth, it nevertheless allows access to a level of perfection which is in itself complete:

> We know full well that God's revelation itself can be received by us only in a human mode; that our intellects can perceive only a

refracted ray of the light; that our humble knowledge through concepts is always analogical, inadequate and relative when we are dealing with mystery; that if God's ways are impenetrable to begin with, his inner mystery is even more so. Nor do we overlook the fact that the inevitable mechanism of objectification always impoverishes the truth that the mind is trying to grasp, and that this truth would indeed be irremediably corrupted if the action of the mind were limited to such a mechanism. But we do not mistake inadequacy for error, or even for inexactness; we also know that a false spiritual dynamism can exist, a morbid fear of objectification, which leaves the mind without nourishment, norms or direction, exposed to every wind that blows. We are not scandalized by the adaptation of the divine light to our human condition. We realize very well that contemplation of the mystery should reduce us to silence; but this silence comes at the end, not at the beginning; it is a silence of fullness and transcendence, not a silence of refusal and emptiness.[60]

This silence reflects, in other words, the barrier which faith experiences when seeking to increase its understanding of God. There is, de Lubac affirms, a level of Christian truth to which humanity is able to gain access, but this does not exhaust the revelation of the Godhead. There is always something beyond the human, the experience of which nevertheless arises in the human.

This human quest for a truth beyond the human is expressed in the notion of doctrinal infallibility. This is a sign of the Church's desire for spiritualization, which evolves as spiritual principles become completely disengaged from compromises with political power.[61] The dogma of doctrinal infallibility is literally a new form of reasoning: 'The proclamation of the gospel in the power of the Spirit brought about a spiritual revolution which created a new mental structure deep within humanity, and, by an imperative logic, this latter, despite some hesitations, had to clear a way to express itself.'[62] The essence of infallibility is not, asserts de Lubac, that the view expressed by the Church is entirely correct, but that it represents the closest earthly approximation to truth and the answer to the prayer of Jesus that the faith of Peter may not fail.[63] The Church, like other communities, from time to time makes legitimate demands for obedience on its members that are not wholly reasonable.

De Lubac is critical of attempts to demonstrate a smooth continuity from philosophical reasoning into theology. He states: 'It was the revelation of the Trinity in its works and by its works that gave to our Creed the essence of its structure.'[64] Similarities in the vocabulary of theology and philosophy might suggest continuity, but de Lubac maintains that words undergo profound changes in meaning, for instance in the theology of Augustine. The bishop of Hippo appropriates various language from Platonist philosophy for the purposes of Christian theology, but neither reduces theology to philosophy nor elevates philosophy to theology. Theology contains a unique element of the revelation of God in Christ, being in the 'most ancient and noble sense' the 'movement of faith, adoration, ecstasy in God'. This symphonic movement is never-ending because God is inexhaustible.[65] It is thus 'liturgical praise and glorification of God'.[66]

Christian philosophy nevertheless persists in three ways. First, Christian belief has impregnated philosophy with axioms on which it has built. Indeed, every philosophical system depends, de Lubac contends, on forms of experience and belief.[67] This is the first sense in which no philosopher can escape from dependence on Christian tradition. Other belief systems which have made equally large contributions, such as those of classical Greece, have also permeated philosophical reflection in similar ways. There are two other ways, however, in which philosophy is Christian, and these are unique. Philosophy, in following these ways, tends towards revelation, becoming conscious of its 'radical insufficiency'. This acceptance and submission of Christian faith to revelation is the 'beyond of philosophy',[68] affecting both philosophy's content and its form of expression. Revelation 'impregnat[es] philosophy in the course of philosophy's work', giving to philosophy, here considered as an objective system, the *content* of revelation, and in particular its guaranteed natural truths and basic principles.[69] Revelation can equally be seen as 'presenting itself to philosophy as its final end', imbuing philosophy, construed as thought and as the *activity* of philosophy, with the '*form* of revelation, of its formally supernatural character and of the truths that participate in this character, inasmuch as they participate in it'. The first consequence of revelation, the supernatural *mode* by which it brings elements into human knowledge, and its second consequence, the *substance* of its claims on humanity, are unified in the human person: from the 'concrete point of view', de Lubac insists, 'all Christian revelation is one.'[70] This is because Christian belief is both a fact of human history, able to be comprehended in human terms, and the absolute truth, the 'mystery through which this revelation will bring the good news to the world'.

These reflections show that philosophy cannot ultimately be regarded as the autonomous exercise of reason which constructs an edifice of propositions proved to be true, or at least not proved false. The fullest Christian definition of philosophy is the 'synthesis of all knowledge, operating in the light of faith'.[71] This definition expresses something of Christian philosophy's contingent character as well as its need of a principle subsisting beyond itself. What should the relation of this form of philosophy be to those which have arisen in the modern world that are, in practice, entirely separated from any revelatory dimension? De Lubac sees Christian philosophy as having the potential to complete such secular forms of rationality, quoting from a manuscript of Pierre Rousselot: 'Our faith is not only the power of believing in certain truths of the supernatural order: it is also, *and at the same time*, a new power of interpreting the visible world and natural being; a renaissance of reason. It is a perfection of the mind, which takes faith up at its foundations, thus restoring, deepening, and enlarging it.'[72]

DOGMA, REVELATION AND DIVINE INEFFABILITY

On 1 November 1950, Pope Pius XII defined the dogma of the Assumption in his apostolic constitution *Munificentissimus Deus*. The Assumption feast had been celebrated for more than a millennium, but the belief that Mary was taken up bodily into heaven had not previously been part of the Church's formally defined teaching. The new dogma was, so the encyclical states, the result of a movement of theology and faith of the whole Church: hope in the minds of individual Christians, crusades of prayer, theological enquiry, and petitions 'truly remarkable in number . . . from every part of the world and from every class of people . . . begging and urging the Apostolic See that this truth be solemnly defined'.[73]

An intuitive capacity residing in the Church as a collective body gives it the competence to discern truths that discursive reasoning alone would be unable to establish.[74] De Lubac describes reason's potential to be illuminated by these truths as its 'conscience' in an analogy with the personal recognition of God described in the previous chapter. The enunciation of these truths, known as the development of dogma and expressed by the teaching ministry of the magisterium, is the prophetic work of the Holy Spirit in the Church, by which human understanding is stimulated and enlightened to develop detailed scientific conceptions of fundamental intuitions. The magisterium is thus the 'permanent norm of all theological activity'.[75] De Lubac says of divine revelation:

> We do not possess it: it possesses us. We do not measure it: we are measured by it. We seek to penetrate into its understanding, and we do in fact reach it: the mystery is incomprehensible, it is not unintelligible. But the more we reach, the more we sense at the same time that this truth surpasses us, that it overflows us and disconcerts us. Each light acquired with respect to it is the cause of a new and more profound obscurity.[76]

De Lubac mounts an uncompromising defence of the place of dogma in religion and society, counselling theologians against lowering the 'horizon of supernatural truth' in attempts to bring religious knowledge into conformity with the expectations of merely human reason. Dogmatic definitions of belief are the result of a defensive reaction against a purely secular use of rationality, which governs both the choice of subjects and their mode of expression.[77] There is a danger that churches with no magisterium will be more inclined to follow social trends and develop patterns of ministry based more on bureaucratic rationality than on the Gospel requirements of Jesus Christ. This is not to say that such churches are necessarily failing to witness to Christian truth, but that it will be harder for them to articulate that truth and agree about elements on which consensus would aid their ministry and mission.

A useful analogy can be drawn between dogma as the Church's collective idea of God, and the idea of God which establishes itself in the minds of individual Christians. De Lubac insists that just as the idea of God is relative to the mind in which it is implanted, and therefore incomplete according to any absolute standard of truth, so dogma is a representation of the Church's own self-understanding at any specific point in time and therefore similarly contingent. He states: 'The error consists in conceiving of dogma as a kind of "thing in itself", as a block of revealed truth with no relationship whatsoever to natural humanity, as a transcendent object whose demonstration (as well as the greater part of its content) has been determined by the arbitrary nature of a "divine decree".'[78] De Lubac sees no fundamental contradiction between the absolute demand which dogma exerts on the believer in Christ, and the inevitably partial nature of the truth of dogma, which is still in course of development. This is because dogma points beyond itself to the truth of God in Christ which is the only complete and objective standard of truth.

One of the most common objections to the truth claims of dogmatic statements is that they fail to recognize legitimate difference of opinion within churches and between them. This objection rests, however, on a misunderstanding of the real nature of dogma. De Lubac states clearly that the Church does not need to provide a comprehensive definition of theological truth, and in fact should not attempt to do so. In the case of debates about the relation between nature and the supernatural, for instance, theologians have rightly been left free to debate the issues involved, and commitment to rigorous theological enquiry in the Church has thereby been enlivened.[79] This is because the ultimate truth about God is ineffable, being too great to be expressed by means of concepts. De Lubac quotes Gregory of Nazianzus's statement that even angels are 'further below the knowledge of God than they are above terrestrial and corporeal natures'.[80] Objections to dogma might therefore arise either from a tendency to extend its doctrinal definitions beyond their proper range of application, or from a false perception that dogma seeks to provide an exhaustive definition of Christian truth claims and leaves no scope for theological debate and diversity.

A further objection to the necessity of a personal individual assent to dogma is founded on a simplistic opposition between opinion and obedience according to which human intellectual autonomy inscribes limits around dogma. In fact, de Lubac avers: 'The distinction between subjective and objective is not entirely acceptable . . . there is an objectivity of the subjective order, because the objective order of revelation is in close correlation with it.'[81] In other words, dogmatic notions as well as those from secular philosophy inform our notion of human individuality and freedom. Another theory of the development of dogma compares Christian truth to a seed, which is present in the Church from the beginning and out of which the Church grows, progressively making explicit the truths which have always lain latent within it. An analogy can be drawn between this theory of dogma and the evolutionary vitalism of Henri Bergson, popular in France in the opening decades of the twentieth century. Bergson's image of the growth of earthly life from a primordial unity into an ever more complex and differentiated whole mirrors the continuity and faithfulness to historic roots which proponents of the 'seed' theory of the origin of dogma typically embrace. De Lubac argues, however, that the seed imagery, despite its apparent dynamism, fails to convey the fact that dogmatic development is a 'progress of revelation'. Employing an evolutionary metaphor, the development of dogma is more like Teilhard de Chardin's theory of creative evolution, in which God acts not so much from the past into the present, but from the *future*, which will be defined by God and given by God, into the present. De Lubac reflects:

> We sometimes reason as if revelation had come simply to add a few bits of knowledge, higher or more hidden, to that which humanity already possessed or that it could at least possess by the fact of its reason. Humans knew, for instance, that God is one: they will henceforth know besides that God is also Trinity. This way of seeing is superficial. The irruption of the Spirit of Christ is something quite different! Revelation, in fact, is at the same time a call: the call to the kingdom, which is not open to humanity without a 'conversion', which is to say, an inner transformation, and as it were, a recasting not only of will but of being itself. Then the entrance into another existence is produced. It is a new creation, which resounds in one's entire awareness: it upsets the original equilibrium, it modifies the orientation of it, it opens up unsuspected depths in it. Eyes open anew onto a new world. The community of a new life allows the giving of a meaning, its whole meaning to the divine object of faith.[82]

Dogma fundamentally calls the whole Church to obedience to divine revelation, rather than individual Christians to obedience to those in positions of higher authority or to those who wish to impose their personal opinion on others. This makes it surprisingly easy to begin to establish ground rules for how theological reasoning in churches should take place. Is it based on attentive and rigorous theological work and reading of Scripture? Does it seek to learn from God's historic self-revelation to the Church in prayer, liturgy and mission? The answers to those questions need to be 'Yes'. Are power or rhetoric being used to silence vigorous respectful debate? Do any participants in the debate believe they have nothing more to learn? The answers to those questions should be 'No'.

Criticism, especially self-criticism, has an important place in the Church. Criticism literally means 'discernment', and good criticism therefore includes within it judgement and choice. It is

a striving for realism in action – a determination to bar all that cannot justify its claim to genuineness. It is an examination carried out in humility, capable of recognizing the good achieved, but arising out of an essentially apostolic discontent and a perpetually restless spiritual dynamism. It is born and grows from attitudes such as the inability to be satisfied with work done and a burning desire for the best; integrity of judgment on matters of method; independence of will to break with customs that cannot be justified any more, to get out of ruts and put right abuses; above all, a lofty idea of the Christian vocation and faith in the mission of the Church.[83]

Criticism of the Church is therefore, at its best, self-criticism. This is not the same as sterile complaining or an unwillingness to place confidence in the Church. All valid criticism is an attempt to plumb the depths of the truth and tradition of faith in Christ by means of attentive and rigorous theological and historical discernment.

De Lubac presents a model of religious knowing in which affirmative and negative moments are simultaneously distinguished and preserved. God reveals himself to humanity but also hides himself from humanity.[84] This dialectic is sustained by God's supernatural action, which preserves a sphere of rational concepts and argument in order to aid humanity in its collective search for truth. Mere repetition and passive remembering are insufficient for living in faith and transmitting that faith to the next generation. Intelligence is also needed to discover anew the truths of faith.[85]

Although there is fundamental discontinuity between philosophy and revelation, this is undermined by the fact that the philosopher and the theologian are one and the same person. Aquinas established both these facts, and in this, de Lubac argues, lies his greatness:

By a process which pure reason alone does not seek to justify, but which the spirit satisfies, or rather insists upon, he was able to penetrate and explore the ways by which the intelligence moves to the point at which he discovered the spiritual appetite within it. In his very philosophy, the philosophical endeavour develops into a mystical flight. The human spirit becomes conscious of its total nature and of its high vocation. He explores all its dimensions, and going beyond the techniques and specializations which obliged him, as it were, to divide himself in two, he seeks to rediscover the simplicity of the mind's essential act. The formal distinctions and oppositions tend to be reabsorbed into unity, although without ever quite reaching it.[86]

De Lubac thus opposes any conception of theological reasoning that fails to recognize the ultimately supernatural character of enlightenment. He does not, however, present the relation between theological reasoning and other forms of rationality as one of simple opposition. In fact, he argues that the theologians of the early modern period who sought to separate nature from supernatural action, such as Cajetan and Suárez, provided the conditions in which not only philosophy but also theology could flourish apart from any intuition of the supernatural. The intellectual process of secularization was thereby advanced. Intellectual secularization possesses, in other words, profoundly theological roots, and is by no means due simply to the impacts made on theology by other disciplines.[87] How can this theological heritage be redeemed and the affirmation of God in human reasoning once again realized? If only the human person synthesizes reason and revelation, then what is needed is human reflection, speech and writing which continually reannounce and celebrate this unity.

CHAPTER SEVEN

CHRIST AND THE BUDDHA

In 1929 de Lubac was appointed Professor of Fundamental Theology in the Catholic Theological Faculty in Lyons. The following spring, the dean of the faculty requested that he add a course on the history of religions to his teaching portfolio for the next academic year. Thus were laid the foundations of his interest in religion in general and Buddhism in particular. De Lubac's engagement with Buddhism developed more fully two decades later. Following the 1950 encyclical *Humani generis*, his books *Surnaturel, Corpus Mysticum* and *De la connaissance de Dieu* were withdrawn from catholic libraries and shops, and he was prohibited from publishing any Christian theology.[1] Buddhist studies enabled him to continue his religious writing and publishing whilst remaining obedient to these restrictions.

De Lubac increasingly focuses his attention on Amidism, or 'Pure Land' (*Jōdo Shū*) Buddhism, rather than the Zen or Tibetan varieties better known in the popular Western mind. Zen is characterized by extreme immanentism: the object of meditative concentration is the self's 'true' nature and its goal the nurturing of the eye of wisdom. In Amidism, however, the Buddha himself becomes the object of contemplation by which the self seeks to inhabit his compassionate heart. As in catholic devotion to Christ, an actual figure is the focus. Furthermore, in Amidism repetition of the name of Amida in the phrase '*Namu Amida butsu*' – a practice known as *nembutsu* – and of his vows, takes the place of the silent, wordless meditation of Zen.[2] This invocation of a personal name is closer to Christian prayer, especially in the Jesus Prayer tradition, than to Tibetan Buddhist yoga or tantra. From a Christian perspective Amidism can thus be seen as the fullest flowering of the *Mahāyāna* (Great Vehicle) tradition, in which meditation and doctrine are represented in a person and a place: the Buddha Amida, and the Pure Land into which the self will be reborn.

THE CROSS AND THE BODHI TREE

The Buddha Shakyamuni instructed his disciple Sarputra that after his death his image should be cut in the shape of a fig tree (*asvattha*) in recollection of his enlightenment gained while meditating under such a tree.[3] The image of the tree as the origin of truth and life appears in several places in the *Lotus Sūtra*.[4] The tree, with its roots in the navel of the Supreme Being, is the 'image and manifestation of this being, the emanation of its energy, the respiration of its breath; it is the symbol of hidden deity; the greatest of the gods reveal themselves as the spirit moving its branches formed of all the elements – air, fire, water, earth.'[5]

In Christian narrative the cross is also described with tree of life imagery, as beautifully depicted in the hymn of Venantius Fortunatus often sung on Good Friday:

Faithful cross above all other
One and only noble tree
None in foliage, none in blossom,
None in fruit thy peer may be.
Sweetest wood and sweetest iron,
Sweetest weight is hung on thee.[6]

The suggestion that the cross is a tree which actually bears foliage, blossom and fruit is reflected in the *khach'k'ar* or 'living crosses' common among Armenian Christians, which have foliage and flowers entwined around them or even growing out of them. The tree motif establishes, moreover, links with other events in salvation history. According to the *Golden Legend* the Cross was hewn from wood from the tree of life in the Garden of Eden.[7] On Adam's death, Seth obtained one of its branches from the cherubim guarding the garden and planted it at Golgotha, named after the skull of Adam who is buried there.

The tree of life therefore represents salvation, in different forms, to both Buddhist and Christian. The salvation offered to the Buddhist is founded on moral self-discipline, concentration and wisdom, and thus possesses pronounced Gnostic overtones. The Buddha experiences suffering simply by his participation in the human condition. He does not, like Christ, take on the suffering of others in order to buy back humanity from sin into fellowship with a divine being distinct from him. There are several similarities between Buddhist and Christian views of salvation, however, notwithstanding this large difference in the nature and goal of the redemptive process. In mainstream Christian soteriology, knowledge also has a key role, being prominent for instance in the Wisdom tradition. There is, moreover, a recurring supposition that the cross was manufactured not from the tree of life but from the tree of the knowledge of good and evil.[8] Furthermore, the motif of spiritual ascent through successive stages of enlightenment is suggested in Christian discourse by the image of the ladder, common in Syriac tradition and inspired by Jacob's ladder of Genesis 28.[9] James of Serugh affirms: 'Christ on the cross stood on the earth, as on a ladder of many rungs.'[10] Christian salvation and enlightenment are nevertheless founded on an event that is necessarily social, and situated within a wider objective history of creation, redemption and future consummation. Buddhist awakening is, in contrast, focused on the self, and when it extends beyond the self empties that self, and the history it inhabits, of reality.

LOVING THE PERSON

De Lubac's interpretation of the figure of the Buddha has implications for both doctrine and anthropology. Just as Christology informs the understanding of the human person, created, redeemed and transformed in the image of Christ, so buddhology cannot be separated from the conception of humanity in Buddhist religion. The central difficulty de Lubac identifies is Buddhism's lack of any developed principle of incarnation.[11] Christ the Word becomes flesh in order to redeem the world, but the Buddha, on attaining enlightenment, transcends the world in a state of *lokottara*. The elevated state which the Buddha comes to enjoy is represented in images from his earlier earthly life. His feet never touch the earth, being raised above it from birth by carpets of lotus flowers, and he is even shielded from the flesh of his mother's womb by a covering of precious stones (*AB* I 116). This is somewhat like a revised Gospel narrative in which Christ always walked on water, removed from the toil and suffering of the world and presenting himself to humankind as a vision, rather than being a concrete person entering fully into earthly human life.

Such doceticism, as de Lubac labels it, can be identified in both Christian and Buddhist traditions, although functions in very different ways in each case. In Christian belief, docetism is traditionally considered heretical, or less negatively, as defining a theological option which lacks coherence. De Lubac's ultimate objection to the notion that Jesus only *appeared* to be human is that humankind would also only appear to be human. But this is exactly the Buddhist position, where doceticism is radical and universal. Amida Buddha inhabits a fictitious body (*nirmanakaya*) that is in reality neither material nor spiritual.[12] De Lubac perceives the wide implications of this understating of divine disembodiment for the material order. The corollary of God not acting on matter and assuming material form is either the Buddhist dissolution of the material order or the scholastic exaltation of materiality as an independently constituted realm of 'pure nature'.

De Lubac's response to the possibility of the dissolution of the created order is his by now well-known concept of the supernatural: divine action, he argues, penetrates, sustains and transforms the whole of creation, which remains entirely dependent on it. He perhaps finds echoes of this relation in the emphasis placed on dependence on Amida in the True Pure Land (*Jōdo Shinshū*) tradition associated with Shinran's disciples, who 'insist even more than Honen's on the feeling of absolute confidence in Amida'.[13] Without this complete dependence there can be no hope of salvation nor even of continued existence. The outcome of the alternative docetic account of the nature–grace relation is, de Lubac suggests, an extreme scepticism which could conceivably be reached by either a Christian route or a Buddhist one: God never entered into the world, his incarnate body was mere appearance, his mouth uttered no true teaching, and written accounts about such teaching are no more than stories.[14] De Lubac in fact suggests that Christian reluctance to accept that God could assume material nature developed under Buddhist impetus: archaeological evidence supports the view that the Nestorian conception of Christ as consisting of two different persons, associated with the East Syrian church, was fostered by religious and cultural exchanges across the central Asian plains during the seventh and eighth centuries.[15]

De Lubac notes that Karl Barth also identifies Amidism as the religious form possessing the most affinity with Christian belief. Yet he critically observes that Barth finds 'scarcely any other difference between the two doctrines of grace than the real efficacy of the name of Jesus Christ . . . without substituting a comparison which would permit a pronouncement on the content of the faiths'.[16] It may be said in Barth's defence that he begins his discussion of Amidism by drawing several anthropological comparisons of the type de Lubac claims are lacking. These culminate in the observation that 'redemption by dissolution' is the goal of Amidism, with the person of Amida, faith in him, and the Pure Land being only means to attaining this goal.[17] Yet Barth characteristically retreats from this cultural–anthropological perspective on Amidist teaching to affirm uncompromisingly that the 'truth of the Christian religion is in fact enclosed in the one name of Jesus Christ and nothing else'. De Lubac ultimately shares Barth's fundamental conviction that theology must be centred on Christ. He also believes, like Barth, that the whole of the created order is dependent on divine action (the 'supernatural') for its preservation, but considers that, in consequence, theological encounter and critique need to proceed with an awareness of the consequences of particular sets of teachings for theological anthropology.

For the Christian, love is transferred from God to the world via the Son in concrete, directed particularity, and the neighbour in Christ is loved in themselves, rather than as a means to further ends. Christian conceptions of charity tend towards universality, in which God's love for the world in the particular gift of his Son becomes the model for the concrete relations of charity which exist between followers of Christ and which impel their mission to persons in the wider world. In Buddhism, however, the self is ultimately an illusion. Charity becomes compassion (*maitri*) directed to alleviate the other's moral or physical sufferings by setting him on the path to spiritual peace and meditation. Compassion is 'declared to be all the more perfect, the more it becomes abstract and generalized', being 'more concerned with suffering in general than with each suffering being in particular'.[18] Buddhist compassion therefore attains its goal not in universality and particularity, but in generality. In Mahāyāna (Great Vehicle) Buddhism the highest form of other-regard is pure, objectless compassion, which finally dissolves into the void of *nirvāna*.

De Lubac traces the origins of this void to the absence in Buddhist teaching of any doctrine of incarnation. The Buddhist, when contemplating their neighbour, does not perceive in them the image of God:

Since in the depths of their being there is no ontological solidity deriving from a creator; since they are nothing but a mass of component parts, with no inner unity, therefore there is nothing in the human being that can call for, or make possible, any ultimate love. Altruism of any kind, whatever its tinge, and however ardent it may be, can only be a procedure for getting rid of desire.[19]

The final end of love for the Buddhist lies in the transcendence of individual selfhood and liberation from individuality and personality. The bodhisattvas themselves provide the model for this state, possessing no real being distinct from the impersonal and unsubstantial buddhahood which absorbs them all in a single *dharmakaya* 'like remote, floating, unreal prefigurings of the Christ'.[20] Buddha does not desire even to remain the leader or director of the community founded by him. His role does not compare with that of Christ, who says of himself 'I am the Way,' and 'Apart from me, you can do nothing.'[21] Christ is 'in his humanity the image of the invisible God. He is his own witness to himself. He presents himself . . . as the object of the faith which he preaches.'[22]

In view of these stark differences in the concept of the self, it is surprising that de Lubac describes both Buddhist compassion (*maitri*) and Christian love as 'charity'.[23] Elsewhere in his theology he employs the term charity in preference to 'love' to describe the Christian vocation because charity suggests a concrete engagement by means of specific loving acts in the world rather than an abstracted state of mind detached from the world. Recognition of the clear distinction between charity and compassion might therefore serve his project better, particularly his later efforts to promote not only social action but mystical awareness as well. Following the Second Vatican Council, de Lubac becomes increasingly concerned to address the decline of the sense of the sacred in the Church. The personal spiritual discipline fundamental to Buddhist compassion aims to cultivate a similar sense, and this type of discipline provides part of the devotional basis for the concrete social action intrinsic to the Christian notion of charity.

What are the implications of de Lubac's critique of the Buddhist dissolution of personhood for the Christian, especially in relation to the concept of love? De Lubac anticipates challenges made to the argument of Anders Nygren in his study *Agapē and Eros* that the truly Christian form of love is *agapē*, a kind of indiscriminately diffused benevolence.[24] Particularly relevant is the distinction already developed by de Lubac's French Jesuit confrère, Pierre Rousselot, between 'physical' and 'ecstatic' conceptions of love. In *The Problem of Love in the Middle Ages*, Rousselot grounds this contrast in the effect of love on its subject and not in any attempt to classify the desire itself.[25] According to the physical conception of love, its end is the preservation and completion of the subject in her love of God, whereas ecstasy brings the subject to stand outside herself in a state of personal disintegration. In too much popular theology, personhood is undermined by pseudo-psychological ideologies of weakness and vulnerability which are the modern equivalent of the ecstatic conception of love, rather than being exalted according to the ancient Christian humanism of the church fathers. De Lubac presents a sustained argument in his engagement with Buddhism that the true vocation of Christian love is to affirm, exalt and complete the physical human person.

FAITH, RELIGION AND CULTURE

De Lubac, writing in 1935, argues that scholars of religion need to free themselves from four perennial 'illusions': that origins common to different religions may be discovered; that the most ancient religious forms can be identified; that primitive religion is the truest religion; and that comparative religion is a pure science rather than the application of a system.[26] Religion needs, de Lubac asserts, to 'disengage from metaphysics'. He considers Buddhist–Christian interaction in terms of *encounter* rather than dialogue in exactly this sense that there is no history or methodology available to formalize the relation. Comments in Clement of Alexandria's *Stromata* have led some scholars to speculate on the existence of a Buddhist colony in Alexandria, but de Lubac points to the distinct lack of evidence for any contact prior to the twelfth century.[27] He regards with similar scepticism the attempt to establish a Buddhist confluence into early Christian teaching via Plotinus's possible sojourn in India.[28]

Different parties to religious encounter nevertheless employ common symbols such as the tree of life. Equally pervasive in religious history has been the legend of Barlaam and his protégé Josaphat, son of the Indian King Avennir, who according to the Christian account was baptized, renounced earthly riches and converted many people to Christ through miracles and preaching. This

legend originates, however, in the life of Siddhartha Buddha composed by Asvaghosa, in which the Buddha forsakes the royal court
in favour of the path of poverty, despite having until then been
sequestered in unmitigated luxury. Although identified with the
Buddha, Josaphat was canonized in the sixteenth century![29]

De Lubac offers a more concrete example of the usefulness to
Christians of narrative and symbolic appropriation. During the era
in Japan when Christians were subjected to state persecution –
which persisted right through the seventeenth and eighteenth centuries and the first half of the nineteenth – the Christians of
Nagasaki and the surrounding district sought the prayers of Mary
before statues of the bodhisattva Avalokiteśvara, known in Japan
as Kannon. Usually represented as a woman, this bodhisattva is
believed to embody compassionate mercy towards the suffering and
to combat the evils that cause it. This devotion to a maternal deity
reflects de Lubac's own catholic and Jesuit respect for Mary the
mother of Jesus.[30] De Lubac remarks: 'The Japanese police saw
only a bodhisattva there: the faithful who invoked her had transformed it into an image of the "Queen of mercy".'[31] These underground Christians (*senpuku kirishitan*) who prayed to the image
handed down their faith from generation to generation, yet their
existence became generally known only after 1873 when the new
Meiji government finally lifted the ban on Christianity. Even today
some hidden Christians (*kakure kirishitan*) continue to exist in the
region practising similar devotions and customs and reading their
own distinctive scriptures.

In this extreme situation of persecution, images used in Buddhist
contemplation fostered the prayer of Christian communities. De
Lubac suggests that the support was made possible by cultural
affinity, identifying a 'certain personalism inherent in the Japanese
turn of mind and far removed from the Indian mentality'.[32] In other
words, the fact that the fullest flowering of Amidism occurred in
Japan needs to be considered in light of cultural constructions of the
human person, which provide the concrete context for religious
belief and are transformed by that belief. Culture not only informs
the essence of belief but shapes the encounter between believers as
well. De Lubac clearly distinguishes the Christian encounter with
Amidism in Japanese culture from the encounter of Christians with
other varieties of Buddhism in the modern West. He argues that
most Christians who have experienced Buddhism have progressed

little further than the 'neo-Western Buddhism' constructed by
Western cultural perceptions of the Orient.[33] In fact, he suggests,
most Western Buddhists have, like Tolstoy, Swedenborg and Wagner,
been more disciples of Schopenhauer than of the Buddha.[34]

Can Buddhism therefore assume truly religious forms in Western
cultures? The notion that de Lubac regards Buddhism as the Eastern
variety of Marxist and fascist atheism is common currency in
English scholarship and originates in Hans Urs von Balthasar's
study of de Lubac.[35] Yet it seems that Balthasar, in making this
assessment, is unusually paying insufficient attention to culture. De
Lubac certainly sees Western transmutations of Indian Buddhism as
preparing intellectual ground for the various forms of totalitarianism that came to occlude them. He refers for instance to a fatal substitution bound up with the 'retreat from scientific rationalism and
liberal democracy, the resurgence of myth, of the arcane, of the
sense of the sacred, of all forms of irrational thought'.[36] His assessment of Buddhism in Asian cultures is, however, more positive. He
states, with reference to both vehicles:

> If religion is defined as a relationship to a personal God, a true
> God, it is clear that Buddhism is not a religion, since it does not
> recognize such a God. It is atheistic. But from a historical and
> descriptive point of view, such a definition of religion is too spe-
> cific. Buddhism leaves no place outside itself, alongside itself, so
> to speak, for anything else that would be a religion. All the func-
> tions of life that are filled by what is commonly called religion –
> that is, functions that are not filled by a pure philosophy or a pure
> moral doctrine – are filled by Buddhism . . . It takes all of human-
> ity, with all of its powers, in order to bring it the total response,
> both speculative and practical, to the question of its destiny.
> Buddhism creates a spiritual link among all of its followers. It
> demands a true 'conversion'. Finally, one senses in Buddhism that
> quivering of the spiritual being in contact with the mysterious
> and the sacred.[37]

The Buddhist and the Christian can thus potentially agree on several
key points of doctrine: the claims to exclusivity of their respective
confessions; the dynamic of call, response, conversion and even
rebirth; the existence of a community of practitioners or believers;
and some kind of sacramental sense.

De Lubac nevertheless remains critical of the absence in Buddhism of any objective, enduring deity. The pure mysticism it espouses leaves, he protests, no place for the living God.[38] Even when represented in the Amidist tradition as infinite light (*Amitābha*), the Buddha remains curiously depersonalized and ultimately dissolves into a void along with all other phenomena. Negativity is a perennial hazard in the Christian tradition as well.[39] To counter it, de Lubac presents a model of religious knowing in which negative moments need to be balanced by positive, cataphatic ones. God hides himself from humanity but also reveals himself to humanity.[40] This dialectic of withdrawal and disclosure makes Christian faith possible, on the basis that its true end is not ignorance but knowledge. Mystery, de Lubac states in his *Medieval Exegesis*, 'carries a strongly objective connotation'. He affirms: 'Mystery is entirely concrete. It does not exist in idea. It does not consist in any atemporal truth or object of detached speculation. This mystery is a reality in act, the realization of a Grand Design; it is therefore, in the strongest sense, even something historical, in which personal beings are engaged.'[41] This mystery is located in the encounter of the believer, constituted as a person in the image of God, with the person of Christ sent by God into the world to transform humanity and the whole of the creation which humankind orders and inhabits.

THE FUTURE OF CHRISTIAN–BUDDHIST ENCOUNTER

The first two drafts of *Nostra aetate*, the Second Vatican Council's declaration on Non-Christian Religions, failed to mention Buddhism. The topic was introduced only once the text had progressed to its third version in November 1964. Buddhism was then identified solely with the experience of *nirvāna*: abnegation and purification of the self as a path to freedom and permanent peace. The fourth and final version echoes, however, de Lubac's more positive and nuanced appraisal, referring to Amida Buddha in its reference to a 'higher source' of illumination beyond that of the self, as distinct from self-centred paths of enlightenment. In Buddhism, 'according to its various forms, the radical inadequacy of this changeable world is acknowledged and a way is taught whereby those with a devout and trustful spirit may be able to reach either a state of perfect freedom or, relying on their own efforts or on help from a higher source [*superiore auxilio*], the highest illumination'.[42]

De Lubac offers his final assessment of the status of Buddhist belief in a paper presented at the Paris meeting of the Secretariat for non-Christian religions in 1971, five years before Balthasar's study of his work was published. It is a more positive appraisal than Balthasar's, and is not taken account of in Balthasar's interpretation of his position. Amidism is grounded, de Lubac affirms, in an 'expression of religious feeling whose value could remain unacknowledged only by a theology that is excessively severe and hardly in conformity with catholic tradition. It is a religious feeling that Christian education, far from destroying, must deepen and lead to its perfection.'[43] This expression of religious feeling should elicit in followers of Christ not an attitude of suspicion but a 'spirit of dialogue' tempered by 'critical regard'. De Lubac defines the latter as an 'effort of true discernment that is as intent on setting aside the distortions coming from negative prejudices as the illusions provoked by generous inclinations'.[44]

De Lubac identifies in Amidism the presence of a 'sentiment of a need for salvation based on a sense of sin increased by the recourse to Amida's grace, without which it is impossible for humanity to be delivered from its sin'.[45] This form of Buddhism is thus characterized by a strong sense of individual salvation, but what it lacks is an eschatological vision of the salvation of the wider world as necessary to this. Even the future Maitreya Buddha, currently awaiting his eventual manifestation, is not the future hope of current humanity so much as the saviour, in a limited sense, of future humanity, being the successor of the current Sakyamuni Buddha. Maitreya therefore has 'no personal interest at all for individuals living today'.[46]

De Lubac here rearticulates the importance of the social and eschatological dimensions of salvation. He states: 'The Christian hope does not aim at a salvation that would be obtained in this world, this spatio-temporal universe within which all of our individual and collective experiences take place.'[47] Salvation is nothing other than the salvation of the world itself, as recognized by Teilhard de Chardin in his evolutionary theology. It is the role of the Church continually to remind humankind of the transcendent social end for which it is destined, which is not part of present immanent reality. In this transcendent end the kingdom of Christ assumes a 'mystical identification' with the Godhead. God for the Christian is, de Lubac states, the 'hidden being par excellence, because he is the personal being par excellence – and, for the one who approaches him, he is the personalizing being'. Amida Buddha is, by contrast, 'reabsorbed in an Absolute transcending all knowledge that can be described only in the most minimal terms of void and space . . . His personality is not sublimated but abolished.'[48]

Attempts have been made over the past 20 years to develop a doctrine of 'engaged' Buddhism according to which salvation has a wide range of practical implications. This inverts the polarities of the historic Buddhist tradition that de Lubac presents: salvation is construed no longer as the transcendence of material existence but as its transformation. Parallels may here be identified with the categories of 'practical' or 'applied' theology in recent Christian thought: these subdisciplines gain their validity from the supposition that they provide methods or conclusions unavailable to 'pure' theology. Two very different transitions are being effected, however. In the case of Christian theology, the new categories are at best superfluous and at worst misleading, suggesting that the fundamental truths of Christian faith contain, in themselves, no practical implications until subjected to additional critical categories and methods. This is false: the fundamental theological truths about creation, incarnation, redemption and salvation are inalienably for the world and transformative of the world. In the case of Buddhism, however, the concept of 'engagement' effects a real transformation rather than a merely apparent one. The idea of 'engagement' does not emerge from historic religious discipline but from the desire to separate that discipline from its dominant traditional cosmology.

The thesis that Amida presents Christian theologians with the most accessible face of Buddhism has been advanced more recently by Galen Amstutz, who states that Amidism 'probably provides the strongest potential point of contact' with the Christian West.[49] The possibility of close study of Amidism in Japan was, however, closed to Western theologians during the sect's period of major flourishing in the isolationist epoch, which lasted from 1641 until the 1860s. Since then, Amidism's distinctive character has typically gone unrecognized and Buddhism has been represented by orientalist narrative as a geographical other: a repository for displaced Western desire and objectification rather than a partner in serious encounter. Critiques of this objectifying approach have developed in the wake of Edward Said's well-known analysis *Orientalism* of 1978.[50] Yet as long ago as 1952, de Lubac deconstructs Orientalist perspectives on

Buddhism and its associated culture.[51] These he terms 'humanist' because they identify particular elements of religions and cultures as possessing universal value on the grounds that they provide historic manifestations of human spirituality and wisdom. They refuse to encounter religions in their full particularity and strangeness.

The paucity of serious studies of Amidism in the countries where it has flourished suggests, however, that orientalism is not only a Western phenomenon. Amidism, being a predominantly rural denomination, can easily be evoked as an historical and cultural other in places in Japan where it previously flourished. Amstutz points to the real difficulties inherent in engagement and critique, arguing that modern scholars have typically omitted to recognize the rooting of True Pure Land Amidism in local communities in contrast with the institutional and monastic organization of Zen and earlier forms of Amidism. He puts forward, moreover, a thesis in the tradition of Max Weber's Protestant ethic that Amidism was vital in the rise of Tokugawa business communities and consequent Japanese economic expansion. Social scientific perspectives such as these help to explain why Amidism has not been so widely translated into Western contexts as Zen, and raise large questions about the extent to which any such translation is likely in the future.

De Lubac's reflections on Buddhism conclude ambivalently. He is frequently critical of the history of the Western encounter of Buddhism and Christianity, whether the syncretism of the legend of Barlaam and Josaphat or the nihilistic pessimism of Schopenhauer. Moreover, he insists, the essence of present encounter cannot be separated from its history and the account of that history. What might the future hold for Buddhist–Christian encounter? Heinrich Dumoulin notes *Nostrae aetate*'s acknowledgement that Christian–Buddhist dialogue 'will take on a different direction and development according to the particular standpoint of the Buddhist partner'.[52] De Lubac's oeuvre reminds those engaged in interfaith dialogue of this fact, suggesting that dialogue should be located in the particularity of the specific denominational and sub-denominational traditions of both Christian and Buddhist belief, and will transform their respective cultural contexts yet also be transformed by them.

EPILOGUE: THE CALL OF THE SUPERNATURAL

On 2 February 1983 when 86 years old, de Lubac was created cardinal deacon of the Church of Santa Maria in Domnica. The building's situation, nestling in the side of the Caelian Hill between the Forum and the Basilica of St John Lateran, reminds the visitor of de Lubac's vision of the Church's own position between classical civilization and the modern world, debate and authority, philosophy and theology, the personal and the institutional. Outside in the Piazza della Navicella stands the statue of a boat, to which he once likened the Church itself 'full of unruly passengers who always seem to be on the point of wrecking it'.[1] This elevation marked for de Lubac the culmination of a lifetime's work for the Church, which had begun with his formation in exile in Britain after the First World War, extended through his spiritual resistance to Nazism in Vichy France, and included a second exile, this time within the Church, during the 1950s. He was excused episcopal consecration owing to advanced years.

What does de Lubac's theology offer the Church and wider society today? We can begin to answer the question by briefly reviewing some important points that have emerged in the course of this book's discussion. The theology of the supernatural reminds us that all events, interventions and miracles in the world are secondary to the single unique gift of the world's creation. It is this great miracle which establishes the whole of humankind in primordial relation with God, in need of divine grace and thus disposed to receive it. The corollary of this insight in political theology is the refusal of any notion of a purely secular state. The Church and its practices are necessarily part of any stable, free society, and civil authorities must provide space for them. This is part of civil society's own divinely ordained function, which churches and people of faith are called to acknowledge. The consequences of undue antagonism between Church and State are summarized in de Lubac's pithy analysis made in 1941 that totalitarianism flourishes when rationalism expels mystery enabling myth to take its place.[2] The supernatural is yet again implicated in the act of faith and subsequent deepening of faith. Humans as reasoning beings have an intrinsic rational orientation towards God, meaning that philosophy is essential to faith but also that faith is more than philosophical apperception. De Lubac is alive to the power of ideas, and of the concepts, creeds and arguments to which they give birth. These call humans both to faithful reasoning, and a reasoning faith.

De Lubac was highly critical of radical liberalizing tendencies ascendant in Church and society during the 1960s. These, he protested, misrepresented the Church's tradition and achievements, esteemed criticism above constructive theology, and sought to erode the Church's hierarchy and diminish its preaching, with their ultimate object being not so much renewal as novelty. It should come as no surprise, he insists, that this ecclesial crisis was in large part a university crisis: ideas are linked inextricably to belief and inform social behaviour. His own response to this crisis was primarily intellectual: the acceptance of a 'pressing invitation to carry through a vast program of research which, despite an incredible mass of work too little known and poorly popularized among the faithful, has not yet attained all the fullness or the hardiness desired'.[3] De Lubac states that, in retrospect, his emphases would have been somewhat different: humanistic values and acceptance of progress, but also the preservation of historic Christian heritage; dogma vivified by the spirit, but equally dogma as the concrete expression of spirit; eternal life being immersed in the present act, but by virtue of this lifting us 'out of the surface level of existence' instead of sacrificing the 'unique essence for the multifaceted current event'.[4] De Lubac, historical theologian par excellence, perceives that theological questions are temporally located even to the extent of being able to regard his own oeuvre as historical.

De Lubac died on 4 September 1991 and his ashes were interred in the simple Jesuit plot in the Vaugirard cemetery in Paris, overlooked on all sides by modern apartment blocks. Consideration of what his response to specific questions facing the Church today might be nevertheless provides ways into a deeper understanding of his theology. His study of scriptural exegesis is, for instance, highly pertinent to current debates. Scripture is used too often as a weapon rather than received as a fount of knowledge, wisdom and belief. This is naturally a violation of Scripture, because it treats the sacred text as a tool with which to pursue individual purposes rather than recognizing the constant challenge it poses to the priorities informing those purposes. The mystical sense of Scripture is, de Lubac reminds us, profoundly concrete, and needs forever to be plumbed. His exposition of the senses of Scripture speaks to contemporary debates about scriptural reading in such contexts as interfaith and feminist theology.[5] Faithful yet imaginative reading, study and proclamation of Scripture are key to these enterprises.[6]

Another area for reflection is the place of humanism in Christian faith. Much of de Lubac's discussion of humanism takes place in the context of his critique of Marxism, and thus demonstrates that humanism, far from being the sole possession of secularizing ideologies, can in fact only be fully realized in the transcendent dimension of human life made concrete by faith in Christ. Yet the present-day European situation is not so much one of a battle between spiritual and nihilist forces as a creeping indifference to any form of transcendental valuation of life. It is also one in which human life is expressed and celebrated in far more diverse forms than in the 1960s, posing new and detailed questions in moral theology that de Lubac does not address.

De Lubac's highly detailed and attentive engagement with Buddhism provides an instructive model for interfaith encounter, being grounded in particularity and extending beyond the three great monotheistic traditions. But what would he have thought about the rise of Islam in his own native France? He might have welcomed a resurgence of public prayer and religious dress within a secularist state. Yet his exposition of how culture and belief are inextricably linked reminds us that when a confessional system is transplanted from one culture into another it is fundamentally changed and needs to be understood in qualitatively new ways. Equally, by showing how culture is a product of religion, de Lubac helps us to understand why attempts by Western corporations and governments to export their ways of life into countries with little Christian history might generate deep and enduring dissonances. His own methodology certainly suggests that interfaith engagement needs to be focused between particular denominations within confessions rather than between people who regard themselves as representing an entire religious tradition. This perspective undermines, moreover, the notion that Christians necessarily have more in common with Jews and Muslims than with adherents of any other confession.

What style of worship might de Lubac lead us towards: a Latin Mass under a baldacchino or a westward-facing celebration with worship songs? His study of Church and Eucharist is on the one hand susceptible of interpretations which seek to diminish a sense of the sacred, and it was indeed his concern in the 1940s and 1950s to counter formulaic and excessively hierarchical patterning of the sacred. Yet he is equally keen to defend the mystical element in worship in the face of excessively informal liturgical styles, and wished to produce a full study of mysticism before his death.[7] The Church as the mystical body of Christ does not supersede the mystical body of Christ in the eucharistic host, but is that mystical body precisely through feeding on the concrete mystical body of Christ in the host. The Mass could accurately be described as a 'holy communion' by virtue of its fusion of these sacred and corporate dimensions.

De Lubac is convinced that wider human society needs this sacred leaven too. The ebbing away of a sense of the sacred in wide swathes of postmodern Western society has, he believes, brought about intellectual, social and emotional impoverishment. When faith retreats from public life and intellectual disciplines no longer concern themselves with claims about ultimate truth, the

> world then becomes a world of abstractions, when it is not absurdly reduced to a world of phenomena. In losing its mysterious innermost depth, it has lost its soul. Humans are isolated, uprooted, 'disconcerted'. They are asphyxiated: it is as if emptiness has been formed in them by an air pump . . . The consequence is not only a social imbalance. The world itself appears 'broken'. There is, at the innermost part of consciousness, a metaphysical despair. It was of this hunger and this thirst that the prophet Amos once spoke: *absolute* hunger and thirst, because they are a futile hunger and thirst *for the Absolute*.[8]

This desire for the absolute can only be satisfied concretely. Christ is the person at once perfectly human and perfectly divine who unifies nature with its supernatural end. It is supremely important that this unification be accomplished in a person, who thus reveals to humankind its own commission of reconciliation. This is the everlasting truth of faith. De Lubac states:

In Jesus Christ everything is accomplished. In him divine revelation is definitively acquired. The Spirit who lives in the Church and animates her as her soul is the Spirit of the Son, the Spirit of the Lord, the Spirit of Jesus . . . He gives us understanding of his Word; he makes it fruitful within us, as he sanctifies us through the effect of his sacrifice. In this twofold sense he continues his task: he brings it to completion. But just as the sanctifying role of the Spirit must not make us misunderstand the absolute objective sufficiency and the unique and definitive character of the redemption accomplished on Calvary, neither should his role as enlightener make us imagine that there can ever be a continuation of divine revelation in the world, as though the revelation given to us in Jesus Christ were only a stage . . . The Spirit of Christ enables us to penetrate into the depths of Christ, but he will never lead us beyond him. He neither speaks not acts 'of himself', no more than Christ spoke or acted of himself; he is sent by Christ as Christ was sent by the Father.[9]

De Lubac warns against separating the Spirit from the Son in order to present the Spirit as a distinct goal of faith, as Joachim of Fiore had sought to do in positing an 'age of the spirit' following the age of Christ and distinct from it. The Spirit proceeds from Christ, and therefore directs faith back to Christ:

The age of the Spirit is in no sense something still to come; it coincides exactly with the age of Christ . . . The Spirit teaches us all truth but neither speaks of himself nor seeks his own glory, any more than Christ, the Father's envoy, sought his own glory. Faithful to the mission he received from him in whose name he was sent to us, he makes us understand his message – brings it to mind – but adds nothing to it. He comes, as it were, to put the seal on his teaching; he opens our awareness to his Gospel but does not transform it. He spoke often before the coming of Christ, but that was solely to proclaim Christ's coming – 'who spoke by the prophets'. And he has continued to speak since Christ returned to the Father; it is all for the proclaiming of Christ's unique lordship and never in order to substitute himself for Christ. In a word, the Spirit is the spirit of Jesus.[10]

The Spirit forever proclaims personality rooted in the mystery of concrete human life and the life of the Church, the mystical body of

Christ. The Joachimite 'third age of the Spirit' in contrast disengages history from the action of Christ through Church and sacraments, thus preparing the way not for the return of Christ, but as Jürgen Moltmann argues, for the *scientific* 'spirit' of the Enlightenment, which de Lubac traces via Rousseau to the twentieth-century totalitarian politics of Marxism and Hitler.[11] He finds alternative models in some unexpected places: the positive eschatology of Vladimir Soloviev, Sergii Bulgakov and Nikolai Berdyaev, and the christology of Teilhard de Chardin. Russian Orthodox theology, less inclined that the Western to see the Spirit as proceeding from the Son as well as the Father, leaves little space for purely spiritualist readings of Christ's activity. Teilhard, acknowledging the modern conceptions of history, progress and biological evolution, seeks to reintegrate these within a renewed theological cosmology in which the whole of creation is enfolded and sustained by the divine action of God in Christ.[12] This is far removed from the modern notion of human progress separated from God and the communion of saints.[13] These theologians all address in their different ways the philosophical and social ideas of their own historical eras and cultures, as de Lubac did his own, in order to reintegrate them within a Christological vision.

De Lubac offers no apologies for conceiving Church and ministry in terms of gender differentiation. This is in his view a direct corollary of the fact that ordained ministers are given to the Church to represent Christ, who serves the maternal functions of the Church as a whole. Whether or not the man Jesus Christ can be represented in the ordained priesthood by women as well as men is a point on which views diverge. In any case, though, de Lubac strongly urges the Church to remain faithful to this representative function of priesthood in both theory and practice, rather than regarding the priest as being for instance primarily a community leader.[14] The Church must remain obedient and receptive to the call of Christ and the discipline of that call, even if it does not always articulate these qualities by identifying itself with Mary and the feminine. It must also retain intact its sense of the personal, which can be eroded by awkward amendments to language in order to eliminate gendered pronouns. De Lubac would agree with feminist theologians who argue that theology has at times in history become too abstract and rationalized, but would not see a further depersonalization of religious language by making it gender-neutral as the best way of countering this trend.

De Lubac leaves his readers with reasons to look to the future with hope. 'People may be lacking in the Holy Spirit,' he acknowledges, 'but the Holy Spirit will never be lacking to the Church.'[15] He records the pessimism of Pope Gregory the Great (in office 590–604) who considered the Church to be in its old age and with nothing left to place hope in except defensive measures protecting it from external threats.[16] Yet such pessimism is, he suggests, based on a category mistake. The ground for hope is Christ, who is everlastingly present to sustain and transform current reality. This action of Christ's is not usually seen in the dramatic rupture of ordinary living presented by Michel de Certeau,[17] but in continual faithful action. Indeed just as the supernatural is always creating, preserving and completing the natural, so the future is forever active on the present to endow it with direction and purpose. De Lubac states:

> The eschatological is not something simply absent from the present, any more than what is transcendent is exterior to everyday reality; on the contrary, it is the foundation of the present and the term of its movement – it is the marrow of the present, as it were, and exercises over it a hidden power.[18]

Discerning hope for the world is a task for all persons of faith and one in which many intellectual disciplines will be implicated. Theology nevertheless has a unique role in this enterprise, relating the whole of life to divine activity and revelation and expressing these by means of coherent ideas and concepts. Its interpretive quest is everlasting: 'Although dogma is essentially unchanging, the work of the theologian is never ended.'[19]

NOTES

INTRODUCTION

1 ASC 19.
2 *Letters of Étienne Gilson to Henri de Lubac* (trans. Mary Emily Hamilton; San Francisco: Ignatius, 1988), p. 188.
3 ASC 42.
4 ASC 35.
5 Marie-Dominique Chenu, *Le Saulchoir : une école de la théologie* (Paris: Étiolles, 1937).
6 BC 251.
7 S 140, 125; cf. AMT 215, 182.
8 'Apologetics and theology', in TF 91–104.
9 ASC 16.
10 ASC 28.
11 Hans Urs von Balthasar, *My Work in Retrospect* (trans. Joseph Fessio and Michael Waldstein; San Francisco: Ignatius, 1993), pp. 11, 89; ASC 47. The Jesuit scholasticate at Fourvière was closed in 1974 when it became part of the Centre Sèvres in Paris. The Catholic Theological Faculty still exists on the rue du Plat. See *Les Jésuites à Lyon, XVIe–XXe siècle*, eds Étienne Fouilloux and Bernard Hours (Lyons: ENS, 2005).
12 ASC 47.
13 S 103, 123, 187; CM 227.
14 S 290, 291.
15 ASC 50.
16 ASC 35.
17 A new edition was finally produced in 1991. See Bernard Sesboüé, « Le surnaturel chez Henri de Lubac : un conflit autour d'une théologie », *Recherches de science religieuse* 80 (1992), pp. 374–408 (374 n. 1).
18 « La question des évêques sous l'Occupation », *Revue des deux mondes*, February 1992, pp. 67–82; discussed in Jacques Prévotat, « Les évêques sous l'Occupation : un démenti du cardinal de Lubac : brèves remarques

sur un document attribué au Père de Lubac », *Communio (French)* 17, 5 (1992), pp. 126–32.
19 ASC 62.

CHAPTER 1: GOD AND NATURE

1 'Aeterni patris', 8; 14, in PE II, pp. 17–27.
2 DG 209.
3 ASC 317–18.
4 PM 285.
5 BC 9.
6 BC 24.
7 S 428, in BC 26.
8 ASC 199.
9 BC 40.
10 Letter to Jacques Maritain, 11 July 1967, archives Kolbsheim, quoted in Dominique Aron, « Une école théologique à Fourvière? », in *Les Jésuites à Lyon, XVIe–XXe siècle*, eds Étienne Fouilloux and Bernard Hours (Lyons: ENS, 2005), pp. 231–46 (232).
11 BC 157.
12 Aquinas identifies the scriptural origins of the vision of God in the *Summa contra gentiles* III, a. 51, 5–6 (5 vols; Notre Dame, IN: University of Notre Dame Press, 1975), III/1, pp. 176–7.
13 For concise summaries of their theologies, see NCE II, pp. 854–5; XIII, pp. 558–9.
14 MS 138.
15 MS 41.
16 AMT 158–9.
17 AMT 51n81; S 487.
18 MS 47–8, 93–4.
19 AMT 2–3.
20 AMT 13.
21 AMT 22.
22 AMT 32.
23 AMT 67–8. NCE I, pp. 892–3 provides a useful synopsis of Jansenius's seminal work *Augustinus*.
24 AMT 68.
25 Rom. 6.18-19.
26 AMT 61.
27 AMT 72.
28 ST Ia, q. 96, a. 2.
29 MS 138.
30 MS 148.
31 MS 7.
32 MS 146.
33 MS xxxv.
34 MS 11, 48.

35 MS 68.
36 DAH 464–5.
37 BC 37.
38 BC 48; quoting Maurice Blondel, *Exigences philosophiques du christian-isme* (Paris: Presses universitaires de France, 1950), pp. 58, 162.
39 BC 85.
40 BC 55; quoting paper of 12 December 1919, *Pierre Teilhard de Chardin – Maurice Blondel: Correspondence*, ed. Henri de Lubac (New York: Herder & Herder, 1976), p. 33.
41 MS 94.
42 MS 76–7.
43 MS 77.
44 MS 236–7.
45 MS 50–2.
46 MS xxxvi.
47 Justin Martyr, *Second Apology* 13, in ANF I, p. 193.
48 TH 405.
49 Tertullian, *Against Praxaes* 5, in ANF III, pp. 600–01; cf. Gen 1.26.
50 MS 20.
51 MS 20–1, emphasis added; from Augustine, *Reply to Faustus the Manichean* 3.3, in NPNF I.4, p. 160.
52 AMT 44.
53 Augustine, *A Treatise on Rebuke and Grace* 10–14, in NPNF I.5, pp. 475–7.
54 AMT 49.
55 AMT 84.
56 MS 26.
57 MS 21.
58 MS 218.
59 MS 95–6; cf. Isa. 65.24.
60 ST IaIIae, q. 111, a. 1, ad 2.
61 MS 58, 229.
62 AMT 174.
63 S 483.
64 MS 84–6.
65 Zech. 1.3, Lam. 5.21.
66 TH 231.
67 MS 183.
68 MS 238; see Eph. 1.3-6.
69 MS 209.
70 AMT 262.
71 TH 227.
72 TH 262–3.
73 TH 252.
74 AMT 265–75.
75 AMT 266–8.
76 DG 186.

CHAPTER 2: SPIRITUAL RESISTANCE TO NAZISM

1 CRA, TF, TH, RCN.
2 Joseph A. Komonchak, 'Returning from Exile: Catholic Theology in the 1930s', in *The Twentieth Century: A Theological Overview*, ed. Gregory Baum (Maryknoll, NY: Orbis, 1999), pp. 35–48 (45).
3 The phrase is well used by Nicholas Atkin, 'The Politics of Legality: The Religious Orders in France, 1901–1945', in *Religion, Society and Politics in France Since 1789*, eds. Frank Tallett and Nicholas Atkin (London: Hambledon, 1991), pp. 149–65 (150).
4 RCN 4.
5 RCN 11.
6 CRA 20, 54.
7 RCN 24.
8 The phrase 'armed peace' is employed in the encyclicals of Leo XIII, *Praeclara gratulationis publicae* (1894) and Pius XI, *Ubi arcano consilio*, 11 (1922).
9 TF 269; see R.W. Dyson, *Giles of Rome on Ecclesiastical Power*, I.3 (Woodbridge: Boydell, 1986), p. 6.
10 TF 203.
11 TF 200.
12 TF 210.
13 TF 211.
14 TF 213.
15 Immanuel Kant, *The Critique of Pure Reason* (Cambridge University Press, 1998), pp. 470–95.
16 US 145.
17 US 151.
18 US 152.
19 US 155.
20 DAH 386–9.
21 Lk. 21. 23b-24.
22 Lk. 22. 49-53.
23 Augustine, *The City of God Against the Pagans*, XIV.28 (Cambridge University Press, 1998), pp. 632–3.
24 TF 251–2, cf. DG 115.
25 TF 219.
26 TF 247.
27 TF 256.
28 TF 266.
29 Ignatius Loyola, *The Spiritual Exercises*, week 2, day 4 (New York: Vintage, 2000), pp. 33–5.
30 P 91.
31 Marsilius of Padua, *Defensor pacis* (University of Toronto Press, 1980).
32 TF 282.
33 US 161, 177–8.
34 DAH 420.

35 DAH 68.
36 « Proudhon contre le 'mythe de la providence' », in *Traditions socialistes françaises* (Neuchâtel: Éditions de la Baconnière, 1944), pp. 65–89 (88).
37 PM 80.
38 RCN 364.
39 MPML 423.
40 SC 186.
41 TH 444.
42 CRA 21.
43 Jacques Prévotat, « Henri de Lubac et la conscience chrétienne face aux totalitarismes », in *Henri de Lubac et le mystère de l'Église* (Études lubaciennes, 1; Paris: Cerf, 1999), pp. 183–208 (193 n. 3).
44 P 95.
45 ST IIaIIae, q. 40, a. 2.
46 TH 437–8. The words of Pius XI were spoken to Belgian pilgrims, 6 September 1938.
47 CRA 67–8.
48 CRA 61, 71.
49 CRA 126–7.
50 CRA 82–102.
51 CRA 91–2. Saul Friedländer, *Pius XII and the Third Reich* (London: Chatto & Windus, 1966), pp. 94–5, reproduces the bulk of the report's text, though de Lubac is critical of the book's wider argument.
52 ST IIaIIae, q. 10, a. 10.
53 1 Tim. 6.1.
54 CRA 99–100.
55 CRA 89. José M. Sánchez, *Pius XII and the Holocaust: Understanding the Controversy* (Washington, DC: Catholic University of America, 2002), pp. 149–53, notes that the Vatican subsequently distanced itself from the report. See also Laurent Joly, *Xavier Vallat (1891–1972) : du nationalisme chrétien à l'antisemitisme d'état* (Paris: Grasset, 2001), pp. 256–9.
56 CRA 144.
57 RCN 404–407.
58 TH 447.
59 TH 502.
60 SC 172.
61 SC 196.
62 TH 450.
63 DAH 263.
64 TH 412.
65 Pierre Teilhard de Chardin, 'The Natural Units of Humanity', in *The Vision of the Past* (London: Collins, 1966), p. 213.
66 US 207, 244.
67 US 254.
68 CRA 190; see *Rerum novarum* 52, in PE II, p. 254; cf. ST IaIIae, q. 93, a. 3, ad 2.
69 US 278–80.
70 Gal. 3.28.

71 RCN 374.
72 RCN 358–9.
73 RCN 358.
74 TH 407, 420–1; cf. Rev. 7.9, Acts 2, Col. 3.11.

CHAPTER 3:   THE CHURCH

1 CF 190–1.
2 'Humani generis' 26, in PE IV, p. 179.
3 ASC 248.
4 ASC 78.
5 In his article « La nouvelle théologie où va-t-elle? », *Angelicum* 23 (July 1946), pp. 126–45.
6 See the discussion « Y a-t-il eu une 'école de Fourvière'? » in Bernard Sesboüé, « Le surnaturel chez Henri de Lubac : un conflit autour d'une théologie », *Recherches de science religieuse* 80 (1992), pp. 373–408 (386).
7 ASC 268.
8 P 171–89.
9 SC 258.
10 RT 56.
11 SC 88.
12 SC 10. De Lubac intended this study as a 'Meditation on the Church', to use the words of its French title. He complained: 'The English translation dressed it up with the pompous title "The Splendor of the Church", which seems to rank it among the "triumphalist" writings and thereby to accelerate its obsolescence.' (ASC 77) The book was published in 1953 purely because the people assigned responsibility for censoring de Lubac's works happened to be absent from Rome at the time the manuscript was submitted.
13 SC 90.
14 Translated as DG.
15 ASC 116–19.
16 C 184.
17 C 184–6; see Gen. 2.9, 6.11–8.19; Lev. 24.1-9; Joel 3.16-17; Heb. 9.4; Josh. 2.1-21.
18 *The Shepherd of Hermas* I.2.4, in ANF II, p. 12.
19 SC 54.
20 SC 110.
21 SC 86.
22 SC 103.
23 Mk 3.14; MC 242.
24 SC 111.
25 MC 91.
26 MC 125.
27 EV 33–40.
28 MP 44.

29 MP 39, 64.
30 MP 43.
31 SC 87–8.
32 SC 202.
33 SC 203.
34 C 103–4, MC 206.
35 CM 268–78.
36 CM 287–8.
37 SC 151.
38 SC 130; cf. 1 Cor. 10.17.
39 SC 132.
40 SC 149. There is evidence that de Lubac comes to see a closer identity between the mystical body of Christ and the Church through successive editions of *Catholicisme*, with two passages on this point being the only revisions subsequent to the fourth (1947) edition. See the note in *Catholicisme* (Oeuvres complètes, VII; Paris: Cerf, 2003), p. xix.
41 Cf. Gregory of Nyssa, *The Great Catechism* 37, in NPNF II.5, pp. 504–6.
42 TF 74.
43 C 96–7, CM 168.
44 CM 256.
45 CM 73, 259.
46 CM 178–9. Augustine, *Confessions* 7.10(16) (Oxford University Press, 1998), p. 124.
47 CM 49–50.
48 CM 66–7.
49 CM 16–18.
50 CM 47.
51 CM 83.
52 CM 117–18.
53 CM 95.
54 CM 154–9.
55 CM 213.
56 CM 220.
57 CM 147.
58 CM 249.
59 CM 251–2.
60 CM 194.
61 RT 65.
62 FT 59; Pierre Teilhard de Chardin, *The Divine Milieu* (Brighton: Sussex Academic Press, 2004), p. 85.
63 FT 125; Pierre Teilhard de Chardin, 'The Mass on the World', in *The Heart of Matter* (San Diego: Harvest, 1974), p. 119.
64 CM 258–9.
65 EF 182.
66 C 63.
67 C 61.
68 MC 190.

69 MC 207.
70 MC 194.
71 MC 210.
72 MC 217–18.
73 MC 199.
74 MC 226, MP 59.
75 MC 218–19, C 296–7; Ignatius of Antioch, *Epistle to the Ephesians* 4, in ANF I, pp. 50–1.
76 MC 222.
77 MC 231.
78 MC 225.
79 MC 226.
80 MC 232; Michael Ramsey, *The Gospel and the Catholic Church* (London: Longman, Green and Co., 2nd edn, 1956), p. 135.
81 MC 275.
82 MC 282; Clement of Rome, *First Epistle to the Corinthians*, in ANF I, pp. 5–21.
83 MC 292.
84 MC 288.
85 MC 288.
86 MC 318; Albano, Frascati, Palestrina, Sabina, Ostia and Velletri, Porto and Santa Rufina.
87 MC 296–7.
88 MC 308–9.
89 MC 90.
90 MC 96.
91 SC 258.
92 MC 254.
93 MC 247.
94 MC 249.
95 MC 273.
96 MC 259.
97 MC 262.
98 MC 313.
99 MC 265.
100 MC 166.
101 SC 140–1.
102 MC 99.
103 MC 101.
104 SC 297, P 95.
105 SC 146, 142, 150.
106 SC 330.
107 SC 333, 336, 346.
108 SC 351.
109 MC 16, 65, 70.
110 MC 158.
111 MC 359.
112 MC 42; e.g. 1 Thess. 2.7; 1 Cor. 4.15; SC 107.

113 MC 131.
114 MC 105.
115 MC 69.
116 MC 72.
117 MC 115; Clement of Alexandria, *The Instructor* I.6, in ANF II, p. 218.
118 C 48.
119 SC 50.
120 SC 219.
121 SC 275.
122 SC 228.
123 C 227.
124 CF 86.
125 CF 187–8.
126 SC 302–9.
127 CF 237.
128 CF 73, 352.
129 C 301.
130 *The Shepherd of Hermas* I.1, in ANF II, p. 9.
131 SC 62–3.
132 C 279.
133 C 323.
134 C 233.
135 C 191.

CHAPTER 4: SCRIPTURE

1 TF 109.
2 ME I, xx.
3 ST Ia, q. 1, aa. 9–10, vol. I, pp. 32–41.
4 TF 125, 123.
5 ME I, 8.
6 ME I, 66, 57.
7 SIT 73.
8 ME I, 48–52.
9 *The Rule of Benedict* (London: Sheed and Ward, 1989).
10 ME I, 29; Ruth 2.
11 ME I, 55–66.
12 ME I, 62.
13 P 107.
14 CF 264.
15 Augustine, *Confessions* 3.5(9) (Oxford University Press, 1998), p. 40.
16 ME I, 44.
17 Clement of Alexandria, *Stromata* I.5, in ANF II, p. 306. This is paraphrase of the Jewish theologian Philo, on whom see HE 150–66.
18 TF 113–14.
19 ME II, 41–2.
20 ME II, 43–4.

21 ME II, 37.
22 ME II, 34.
23 TF 116.
24 ME II, 179.
25 SC 159.
26 ME II, 52.
27 Augustine, *The Advantage of Believing* 3(5–9), in *The Fathers of the Church* 4 (Washington, DC: Catholic University of America Press, 1992), pp. 396–402.
28 1 Cor. 10.11.
29 ME II, 26.
30 ME II, 20.
31 ME II, 93–4.
32 ME II, 21.
33 ME II, 9. See 'Hellenistic Allegory and Christian Allegory', in TF 165–96.
34 ME II, 5.
35 Gal. 4.24-26.
36 ME II, 18.
37 ME II, 55.
38 ME I, 229.
39 TH 446–7.
40 Gen. 3.8; Isa. 65.25; Mt. 5.29; Mt. 4.8; ME II, 13–14.
41 ME I, 80–1.
42 ME II, 63.
43 ME II, 108.
44 ME II, 86; Augustine, 'Sermon 45' on Mk 8.1-9 (Feeding the Four Thousand) 3, in NPNF I.6, p. 406.
45 ME II, 88.
46 ME II, 112–13.
47 Gen. 19.30-38; 2 Sam. 11.
48 ME II, 64.
49 Pseudo-Dionysius, *Celestial Hierarchy* II.2-3, in *The Complete Works* (New York: Paulist, 1987), pp. 148–50.
50 ME II, 150.
51 ME II, 156.
52 ME II, 160.
53 ME II, 129.
54 ME II, 134.
55 ME I, 114–15.
56 ME II, 31.
57 ME I, 131, 121.
58 ME II, 132.
59 ME I, 146.
60 ME I, 78.
61 ME II, 132.
62 ME II, 132.
63 ME II, 133.
64 ME II, 138, 140.

65 ME II, 142.
66 ME II, 129.
67 ME II, 140.
68 ME II, 141.
69 ME II, 181.
70 ME II, 183.
71 ME II, 186.
72 ME II, 187.
73 ME II, 197.
74 ME II, 204–5.
75 SIT 50.
76 SIT 52.
77 ME I, 235.
78 ST 175, 178, 182.
79 CRA 103–16.
80 SIT 9.
81 SIT 37.
82 SIT 44.
83 ME II, 98.
84 MP 17.
85 C 171–2.
86 ME II, 101.
87 SIT 217.
88 SIT 27, 53.
89 ME II, 123.
90 Lk. 4.16-21, 24.27, 24.44.
91 Acts 2.14-36, 7.2-53, 13.26-37.
92 ME I, 24.
93 TF 125.
94 TF 117, ME I, 95, 133.
95 ME I, 237; Rev. 5.5.
96 ME I, 239.
97 SIT 182–94.

CHAPTER 5: PERSON, WORLD AND HISTORY

1 CF 237.
2 C 166.
3 Augustine, *On the Psalms* 68.2, in NPNF I.8, p. 286. God reveals every-where the effects of his presence.
4 C 169.
5 C 204.
6 Introduction to Origen, *On First Principles* (New York: Harper Torchbook, 1966), p. x.
7 C 205; Origen, *Homilies on Luke* 34.3, in *Homilies on Luke. Fragments on Luke* (Fathers of the Church, 94; Washington, DC: Catholic University Press of America, 1996), p. 138.

8 C 140–1.
9 cf. Rev. 22.13.
10 PM 137.
11 C 166.
12 C 29–30.
13 C 38–9; Gregory of Nyssa, *On the Making of Man* 16.18, in NPNF II.5, p. 406.
14 Rom. 8.
15 TH 121.
16 Plato, *Phaedrus* 246a–b, 253c–e (Harmondsworth: Penguin, 1973), pp. 50–1, 61–2.
17 TH 122; Origen, *Against Celsus* 1.5, in ANF IV, p. 396.
18 Deut. 6.5.
19 Ps. 16.9.
20 1 Thess. 5.23.
21 TH 117.
22 Origen, *De principiis* I.3.4.1, in ANF IV, p. 253.
23 TH 125.
24 Philo, *Allegorical Interpretation of Genesis* 1.12, in *Works* I (11 vols: London: Heinemann, 1949), pp. 166–9.
25 Gen. 2.7.
26 TH 136.
27 Jn 20.22.
28 TH 180.
29 The expression is from John Milbank, *The Suspended Middle: Henri de Lubac and the Debate Concerning the Supernatural* (London: SCM, 2005); and in turn from Hans Urs von Balthasar, *The Theology of Henri de Lubac* (San Francisco: Ignatius, 1991), p. 15. Balthasar does not attribute a source, but Pierre Teilhard de Chardin had written to de Lubac many years earlier: 'The whole theory of the supernatural . . . asserts itself in a sphere of thought that most moderns have deserted . . . We are totally and essentially *suspended* by divine attraction.' Letter of 27 June 1934, in *Lettres intimes à Auguste Valensin, Bruno de Solages, Henri de Lubac, André Ravier, 1919–1955*, ed. Henri de Lubac (Paris: Aubier-Montaigne, 1972), pp. 277–8, original emphasis. This collection includes 23 of Teilhard's letters to de Lubac from the period 1930 to 1949.
30 TH 194.
31 C 332.
32 TH 405.
33 C 226.
34 MC 280.
35 C 142.
36 FT 124.
37 C 209.
38 PM 216; Maurice Blondel, *Action* (Notre Dame, IN: University of Notre Dame Press, 2003), p. 101.
39 ST Ia, q. 96, a. 2.

40 PM 336, 167.
41 RT 127–8; Pierre Teilhard de Chardin, 'Operative Faith', in *Writings in Time of War* (London: Collins, 1968), p. 242.
42 RT 127; Irenaeus, *Against the Heresies* IV.5.1, in ANF I, p. 466.
43 Heb. 4.12.
44 PM 179.
45 CF 112, 88.
46 CF 112.
47 TH 141, 129; 1 Cor. 2.11.
48 TH 138; Origen, *Commentary on the Gospel of Matthew* 13.2, in ANF 10, pp. 475–6.
49 FT 125.
50 Teilhard de Chardin, 'The Priest', in *Writings in Time of War*, p. 205.
51 Teilhard de Chardin, 'The Mass on the World', in *The Heart of Matter* (San Diego: Harvest, 1974), p. 119.
52 RT 159.
53 PM 277–8.
54 Pico della Mirandola, *On Being and the One* 8, in *On the Dignity of Man. On Being and the One. Heptaplus* (Indianapolis: Hackett, 1998), p. 58.
55 PM 296–7; Pico della Mirandola, *Heptaplus* V.7, pp. 137–8.
56 Col. 1.17.
57 CF 282.
58 CF 285.
59 MC 141.
60 CF 87.
61 CF 282–3.
62 CF 83.
63 MC 143.
64 C 362.
65 John Webster, *Karl Barth* (London: Continuum, 2nd edn, 2004), p. 166.
66 TH 128.
67 Karl Barth, *Church Dogmatics* (10 vols; Edinburgh: T&T Clark, 1936–77), III/1, pp. 237, 249.
68 Barth, *Church Dogmatics,* III/2, p. 355.
69 Aristotle, *Metaphysics* XII.9 (London: Penguin, 1998), p. 383.
70 DAH 20, DG 13.
71 DAH 20, PM 167.
72 Gregory of Nyssa, *Commentary on the Song of Songs* (Brookline, MA: Hellenic College Press, 1987), Homily II, p. 69.
73 DAH 23; Clement of Alexandria, *Exhortation to the Heathen* 11, in ANF IV, pp. 102–4.
74 DAH 12.
75 DAH 25.
76 DAH 78. The conflict between Apollonian and Dionysian principles provides the governing theme of *The Birth of Tragedy* (Oxford University Press, 2000).

77 DAH 129.
78 TH 495.
79 TH 499.
80 PM 224, 155.

CHAPTER 6:   FAITH, BELIEF AND REASON

1 TF 428; Paul Claudel, *I Believe in God: A Meditation on the Apostles' Creed*, I.I (San Francisco: Ignatius, 2002), p. 38.
2 CF 318–19.
3 The original article is translated in *The Eyes of Faith. Answer to Two Attacks* (New York: Fordham University Press, 1990), pp. 19–82.
4 See Avery Dulles, 'Principal theses of the position of Pierre Rousselot', in Rousselot, *Eyes of Faith*, p. 113.
5 « Deux Augustiniens fourvoyès : Baïus et Jansénius », *Recherches de science religieuse* 21 (1931), pp. 422–43, 513–40, provided the two opening chapters of *Surnaturel*.
6 CF 275.
7 DG 54.
8 DG 12, 168.
9 TF 100, cf. TH 405.
10 Tertullian, *The Apology* 17, in ANF III, p. 32.
11 MPML 423.
12 DG 40.
13 DG 12–13.
14 DG 32.
15 DG 69.
16 DG 99.
17 DG 76.
18 CF 142–3.
19 Jas 2.18-19.
20 CF 141; Augustine, *Homilies on the Gospel of John* 29.6, in NPNF I.7, p. 185.
21 CF 165–6.
22 SC 33.
23 SC 36.
24 CF 146–7.
25 CF 147.
26 SC 15.
27 DG 62.
28 DG 106.
29 DG 150.
30 DG 73–4, 116.
31 DG 39.
32 DG 55.
33 DG 168.
34 TH 56; Pascal, *Pensées* 201 (London: Penguin, rev. edn, 1995), p. 66.

35 TH 52.
36 DG 190.
37 DG 181.
38 DG 192.
39 TH 521.
40 TH 523.
41 TH 543.
42 Pierre Teilhard de Chardin, 'My Fundamental Vision', in *Toward the Future* (San Diego: Harvest, 1973), p. 188.
43 DG 195.
44 DG 112.
45 TF 378.
46 Maurice Blondel, *Action: Essay on a Critique of Life and a Science of Practice* (Notre Dame, IN: University of Notre Dame Press, 2003).
47 TF 403.
48 DG 117.
49 DG 134; Maximus the Confessor, *Capita theologicae et oeconomicae* 1.31.
50 DG 10.
51 RF 83.
52 OCP 483–4.
53 Anselm, *Proslogion*, 16 (Notre Dame, IN: University of Notre Dame Press, 1979), p. 137.
54 RF 105.
55 RF 93–4, CM 237–8.
56 CF 255.
57 CF 256.
58 DG 138–41.
59 TF 216.
60 CF 322.
61 TF 217.
62 CF 277.
63 MP 76–7; Lk. 22.31-32.
64 CF 131.
65 CF 314.
66 CF 327.
67 OCP 484.
68 OCP 487–8.
69 OCP 490.
70 OCP 491.
71 OCP 497.
72 OCP 498–9.
73 *Munificentissimus Deus* 6–9 (Dublin: Irish Messenger, 1951), p. 5.
74 TH 251.
75 SC 29.
76 TH 265.
77 C 311.
78 TH 93.

79 AMT 266–8.
80 Gregory of Nazianzus, *Oration* 28.3, in NPNF II.7, p. 289.
81 TH 269–70.
82 TH 275.
83 SC 284–5.
84 DG 138–41.
85 P 23.
86 DG 153–4.
87 AMT 264–5.

CHAPTER 7:   CHRIST AND THE BUDDHA

1 ASC 74.
2 AB II, 14; ch. 7.
3 AB I, 57.
4 *Lotus Sūtra* 7; 27.
5 AB I, 65.
6 AB I, 60.
7 Jacobus de Voragine, 'The Exaltation of the Holy Cross', in *The Golden Legend*, I (2 vols; Princeton, NJ: Princeton University Press, 1993), pp. 168–73.
8 AB I, 58.
9 AB I, 61–2.
10 'Homily on the Vision of Jacob at Bethel', 95.
11 AB I, 37.
12 AB I, 119.
13 TF 351, AB II, ch. 9.
14 AB I, 120.
15 TF 289–307, AB II, ch. 10.
16 AB II, 7.
17 Karl Barth, *Church Dogmatics* (10 vols; Edinburgh: T&T Clark, 1936–77), I/2, pp. 340–3. See Charles Waldrop, 'Karl Barth and Pure Land Buddhism', *Journal of Ecumenical Studies* 24 (1987), pp. 574–97.
18 AB I, 38.
19 AB I, 41.
20 AB I, 49.
21 AB II, 5; Jn 14.6, 15.5.
22 AB II, ch. 11.
23 AB I, 52.
24 Anders Nygren, *Agapē and Eros* (London: SPCK, 1982).
25 Pierre Rousselot, *The Problem of Love in the Middle Ages: A Historical Contribution* (Milwaukee, WI: Marquette University Press, 2001); trans. of *Pour l'histoire du problème de l'amour au moyen âge* (Munster: Aschendorff, 1908).
26 TF 317.
27 RBO 19, 32.
28 RBO 24, 202.

29 RBO 28–31. For the Christian version, see de Voragine, 'Saints Barlaam and Josaphat', in *Golden Legend*, II, pp. 355–66.
30 MC, EF.
31 AB II, ch. 5, TF 359–60.
32 AB II, ch. 11.
33 RBO 208.
34 RBO 280.
35 Hans Urs von Balthasar *The Theology of Henri de Lubac: An Overview* (San Francisco: Ignatius, 1991), pp. 54–9.
36 RBO 242.
37 TF 333–4.
38 RBO 279.
39 RBO 282.
40 DG 138–41.
41 ME II, 20, 93–4.
42 'Declaration on the Church's Relation to Non-Christian Religions', 2, in *Decrees of the Ecumenical Councils*, II (2 vols; London: Sheed & Ward, 1990), p. 969. See Mikka Ruokanen, *The Catholic Doctrine of Non-Christian Religions According to the Second Vatican Council* (Leiden: Brill, 1992), pp. 124–8.
43 TF 359.
44 TF 363.
45 TF 365.
46 TF 371–3.
47 TF 366.
48 TF 368.
49 Galen Amstutz, *Interpreting Amida: History and Orientalism in the Study of Pure Land Buddhism* (Albany: State University of New York Press, 1997), p. 121.
50 Edward Said, *Orientalism* (London: Routledge and Kegan Paul, 1978).
51 RBO 262–8.
52 Heinrich Dumoulin, 'Excursus on Buddhism', in *Commentary on the Documents of Vatican II*, ed. Herbert Vorgrimler (5 vols; London: Burns & Oates, 1967–9), III, pp. 146–50.

EPILOGUE

1 SC 112–13.
2 TH 444.
3 'The Church in Crisis', *Theology Digest* 17 (1969), pp. 312–25 (323).
4 'Retraction', MP 97–8.
5 Peter Ochs, 'Scripture', in *Fields of Faith: Theological and Religious Studies for the Twenty-First Century*, eds David Ford, Janet Soskice and Ben Quash (Cambridge University Press, 2004), pp. 114–17; Grace Jantzen, 'The Mystical Meaning of Scripture: Medieval and Modern Presuppositions', *King's Theological Review* 11, 2 (1988), pp. 39–43.

6 Hans Urs von Balthasar, *My Work in Retrospect* (San Francisco: Ignatius, 1993), pp. 97–102, discussing P and MP.
7 ASC 113.
8 TH 443.
9 CF 247–8.
10 SC 207.
11 PS II, 443, S 140.
12 PS II, 406–34.
13 PS I, 357.
14 John Thurmer, *The Son in the Bible and the Church* (Exeter: Paternoster, 1987) provides a cogent defence of the representational model.
15 SC 235.
16 C 227; Gregory the Great, *Morals on the Book of Job*, 19.12(19) (4 vols; Oxford: Parker, 1844–50), II, pp. 409–10.
17 PS II, 447–8.
18 SC 117.
19 C 325.

BIBLIOGRAPHY AND ABBREVIATIONS

WORKS BY HENRI DE LUBAC

Publication of de Lubac's *Oeuvres complètes*, (50 vols; Paris: Cerf, 1998–), is in progress. Many of his major works are now available in English translation, and these are cited where available, along with the original French title in cases where the English is not a literal translation. The international Catholic journal *Communio*, which de Lubac was instrumental in founding, has made available translations of some important essays. All references are made to the English-language edition unless otherwise specified.

AB I   *Aspects of Buddhism*, trans. George Lamb, vol. 1; London: Sheed & Ward, 1953. The opening chapter 'Buddhist Charity and Christian Charity' is reprinted in *Communio* 15, 4 (1988), pp. 497–510.

AB II   *Aspects du bouddhisme*, vol. 2: *Amida*; Paris: Seuil, 1955; trans. Amita Bhaka, *History of Pure Land Buddhism, Buddha Dhyana Dana Review* 12, 5–6 (2002); 13, 1 (2003), at www.bdcu. org.au/BDDR.

AMT   *Augustinianism and Modern Theology*, trans. Lancelot Sheppard, New York: Crossroad, 2000. Closely follows part one of *Surnaturel*.

ASC   *At the Service of the Church: Henri de Lubac Reflects on the Circumstances that Occasioned his Writings*, trans. Anne Englund Nash, San Francisco: Ignatius, 1993. An invaluable memoir.

BC   *A Brief Catechesis on Nature and Grace*, trans. Richard Arnandez, San Francisco: Ignatius, 1984.

C   *Catholicism: Christ and the Common Destiny of Man*, trans. Lancelot Sheppard and Anne Englund Nash, San Francisco: Ignatius, 1988. Translation of the fourth edition (1947) with appendix and virtually identical to the final seventh edition (1983).

CF   *The Christian Faith: An Essay on the Structure of the Apostles' Creed*, trans. Richard Arnandez, San Francisco: Ignatius, 1986.

CM	*Corpus Mysticum*, trans. Gemma Simmonds, London: SCM, 2006.
CRA	*Christian Resistance to Anti-Semitism: Memories from 1940–1944*, trans. Anne Englund Nash, San Francisco: Ignatius, 1990.
DAH	*The Drama of Atheist Humanism*, San Francisco: Ignatius, 1995. Translation by Edith Riley, Anne Englund Nash and Mark Sebanc of the 1983 edition including chapters omitted from the 1949 translation.
DG	*The Discovery of God*, Edinburgh: T&T Clark, 1996. Translation by Alexander Dru with Mark Sebanc and Cassian Fulsom of *Sur les chemins de Dieu*, which is an enlarged edition of *De la connaissance de Dieu*.
EF	*The Eternal Feminine: A Study on the Poem by Teilhard de Chardin*, trans. René Hague, London: Collins, 1971.
EV	*Entretien autour de Vatican II : souvenirs et réflexions*, Paris: Cerf, 1985.
FT	*The Faith of Teilhard de Chardin and Note on the Apologetics of Teilhard de Chardin*, trans. René Hague, London: Burns & Oates, 1965. Includes translation of *La Prière de Teilhard de Chardin*.
HE	*Histoire et l'esprit : l'intelligence de l'Écriture d'après Origène*, Oeuvres complètes, 16; Paris: Cerf, 2002. Chs 1–2 are translated as the introduction to Origen, *On First Principles*, New York: Harper Torchbook, 1966, pp. vii–xxii, and the conclusion in SIT, pp. 1–84.
MC	*The Motherhood of the Church*, trans. Sergia Englund, San Francisco: Ignatius, 1982. Includes *Particular Churches in the Universal Church*.
ME	*Medieval Exegesis*, vol. 1 trans. E.M. Macierowski, vol. 2 trans. Mark Sebanc; Edinburgh: T&T Clark, 1998– . Incomplete translation of *L'Exégèse médiévale : les quatre sens de l'Écriture*, 4 vols; Paris: Aubier-Montaigne, 1959–64. The four senses of Scripture are expounded most clearly in vol. II. SIT, pp. 173–217, translates vol. III, chs 2.3 (part) and 2.5 (part); and IV, ch. 7.5.
MP	*More Paradoxes*, San Francisco: Ignatius, 2002. Translation by Anne Englund Nash of *Autres paradoxes*.
MPML	'A Meditation on the Principle of the Moral Life', trans. Adrian Walker, *Communio* 26, 2 (1999), pp. 418–28; originally in *Revue apologétique* 65 (1937), pp. 257–66.
MS	*The Mystery of the Supernatural*, trans. Rosemary Sheed, New York: Crossroad, 1998.
OCP	'Retrieving the Tradition: On Christian Philosophy', trans. Sharon Mollerus and Susan Clements, *Communio* 19, 3 (1992), pp. 478–506.
PF	*Paradoxes of Faith*, San Francisco: Ignatius, 1987. Combines volumes previously published as *Paradoxes* and *Further Paradoxes*, which were translations of *Paradoxes* by Paule Simon and Sadie Kreilkamp and *Nouveaux paradoxes* by Ernest Beaumont.
PM	*Pic de la Mirandole : études et discussions*, Paris: Aubier-Montaigne, 1974.

PS   *La Postérité spirituelle de Joachim de Flore*, 2 vols.; Namur: Culture et vérité, 1979–81.

RBO   *La Rencontre du bouddhisme et de l'Occident*, Oeuvres complètes, 22; Paris: Cerf, 2000.

RCN   *Résistance chrétienne an nazism.* Oeuvres complètes 34, Paris: Cerf, 2006. Includes CRA and 18 articles.

RF   *Recherches dans la foi : trois études sur Origène, saint Anselme et la philosophie chrétienne*, Paris: Beauchesne, 1979. The third essay is a light revision of « Sur la philosophie chrétienne », *Nouvelle revue théologique* 63 (1936), pp. 225–53, translated as OCP.

RS   *La Résistance spirituelle, 1941–1944 : les cahiers clandestins du Témoignage chrétien*, Paris: Albin Michel, 2001. This is an edited version of *Cahiers et courriers clandestins du Témoignage chrétien: 1941–1944*, ed. Renée Bédarida, Paris: Éditions ouvrières, 1977.

RT   *The Religion of Teilhard de Chardin*, trans. René Hague, London: Collins, 1970.

S   *Surnaturel : études historiques*, Paris: Desclée, 2nd edn, 1991. Part one is closely followed in AMT, and the conclusion translated by David Coffey in *Philosophy and Theology* 11, 2 (1999), pp. 368–80.

SC   *The Splendor of the Church*, San Francisco: Ignatius, 1986. Translation by Michael Mason of *Méditation sur l'Église*.

SIT   *Scripture in the Tradition*, trans. Luke O'Neill, New York: Crossroad, 2000. This collection was first published as *Sources of Revelation*. It comprises the conclusion of HE (pp. 1–84); ME I, ch. 5 (pp. 85–158); II, chs 8.3 and 10.3, III, chs 2.3 (part) and 2.5 (part), IV, ch. 7.5 (pp. 159–229).

TF   *Theological Fragments*, San Francisco: Ignatius, 1989. Translation by Rebecca Howell Balinski of the collection of essays *Théologies d'occasion*, with topics including scriptural exegesis, Church–State relations and Buddhism.

TH   *Theology in History*, trans. Anne Englund Nash, San Francisco: Ignatius, 1996. A collection of essays on topics including Christian anthropology and spiritual resistance to Nazism, omitting the bibliography from the French edition.

US   *The Un-Marxian Socialist: A Study of Proudhon*, trans. R.E. Scantlebury, London: Sheed & Ward, 1948.

Note on other works

Several of de Lubac's works comprise papers presented at conferences around the period of the Second Vatican Council, or are based on such papers. The important material from most of these works is included in other more systematic expositions, but these works remain valuable for conveying a sense of the context in which de Lubac refined and communicated his theology. *The Church: Paradox and Mystery* (trans. James Dunne; New York: Alba House, 1969), includes two texts delivered in March and September 1966 at Notre Dame, Indiana, and in Rome. *Athéisme et sens de l'homme : une double requête de 'Gaudium et Spes'* (Paris: Cerf, 1968) is a developed version of a report presented in Chicago. *Dieu se dit dans l'histoire* (Paris: Cerf, 1974), first published as part of a comprehensive collection of conciliar texts in 1968, is a commentary on *Dei verbum*, the Dogmatic Constitution on Revelation. *Teilhard et notre temps* (Paris: Aubier, 1971) is an address given in Toronto, originally published in 1968 as an appendix to EF. *L'Église dans la crise actuelle* (Paris: Cerf, 1969) is an expanded version of an address given in St Louis, Missouri. *The Motherhood of the Church*, first published in 1971, resulted from a conference in Venice, and includes *Particular Churches in the Universal Church*, which formed a response to a request for doctrinal exposition from the Sacred Congregation for the Propagation of the Faith (now the Congregation for the Evangelization of Peoples). See also Christopher Walsh, 'Henri de Lubac in Connecticut: Unpublished Conferences on Renewal in the Postconciliar Period', *Communio* 23, 4 (1996), pp. 786–805.

Reference works

ANF   *Ante-Nicene Fathers of the Christian Church*, 10 vols; Grand Rapids, Mich.: Eerdmans, 1993.

NCE   *New Catholic Encyclopaedia*, 15 vols; Detroit: Gale, 2nd edn, 2003.

NPNF   *Nicene and Post-Nicene Fathers of the Christian Church*, 28 vols; Grand Rapids, Mich.: Eerdmans, 1961.

PE   *The Papal Encyclicals*, 5 vols; Pierian: Ann Arbor, 1990.

ST   Thomas Aquinas, *Summa theologiae*, 60 vols; London: Blackfriars, 1962–76.

WORKS ABOUT HENRI DE LUBAC

The quantity of expository work on de Lubac in English is limited. Hans Urs von Balthasar's *The Theology of Henri de Lubac: An Overview* (trans. Joseph Fessio and Michael Waldstein; San Francisco: Ignatius, 1991), based on the 1976 German original, provides a brief overview of some elements of de Lubac's theology. Joseph Komonchak's article 'Theology and Culture and mid-Century: The Example of Henri de Lubac', *Theological Studies* 51 (1990), pp. 579–602, assesses de Lubac's intellectual context and agenda. The following suggestions for further reading, which are not intended as a complete bibliography, include the most accessible scholarly work for readers of English under each chapter heading.

1. God and nature

John Milbank, *The Suspended Middle: Henri de Lubac and the Debate Concerning the Supernatural* (London: SCM, 2005) draws de Lubac into encounters with Aquinas, von Balthasar and French phenomenology. This is an expanded version of his essay in *The Modern Theologians*, eds David Ford with Rachel Muers (Oxford: Blackwell, 3rd edn, 2005), pp. 76–91. Bruno Forte, 'Nature and Grace in Henri de Lubac: From *Surnaturel* to *Le Mystère du surnaturel*', *Communio* 23, 4 (1996), pp. 727–37, introduces this difficult but central area of de Lubac's theology. Peter J. Leithart, 'Marcionism, Postliberalism, and Social Christianity', *Pro Ecclesia* 8, 1, pp. 85–97, provides a provocative assessment, and Alfred Vanneste, *Nature et grâce dans le théologie occidentale : dialogue avec H. de Lubac* (Leuven: Peeters, 1996) is a detailed historical-critical study.

2. Spiritual resistance to Nazism

Jacques Prévotat, « Henri de Lubac et la conscience chrétienne face aux totalitarismes », and Renée Bédarida, « Théologie et guerre idéologique », in *Henri de Lubac et la mystère de l'Église* (Études lubaciennes, 1; Paris: Cerf, 1999), pp. 183–208, 209–18, give informed accounts. De Lubac's own memoir ASC remains the principal source.

3. The Church

Paul McPartlan, *The Eucharist Makes the Church: Henri de Lubac and John Zizioulas in Dialogue* (Edinburgh: T&T Clark, 1996) is an excellent comparative study, and Susan Wood, *Spiritual Exegesis and the Church in the Theology of Henri de Lubac* (Grand Rapids, Mich.; Eerdmans/Edinburgh: T&T Clark, 1998) provides a complementary perspective. Gianfranco Coffele, 'De Lubac and the Theological Foundation of the Missions', *Communio* 23, 4 (1996), pp. 757–75, and Christopher Walsh, 'De Lubac's Critique of the Postconciliar Church', *Communio* 19, 3 (1992), pp. 404–32, focus on other areas. 'Barth in dialogue: Henri de Lubac on the Church', in Joseph Mangina, *Karl Barth: Theologian of Christian Witness* (Aldershot: Ashgate, 2004), pp. 164–72, supplies comparison. ASC provides extensive details of the controversies surrounding de Lubac's work in the period 1946–1960, and EV offers insights into his role at the Second Vatican Council. A useful collection is *Henri de Lubac: la rencontre au coeur de l'Église*, ed. Jean-Dominique Durand (Paris: Cerf, 2006).

4. Scripture

Susan Wood's *Spiritual Exegesis and the Church*, pp. 22–51, provides a useful summary of the four senses of scripture, as does William Murphy, 'Henri de Lubac's Mystical Tropology', *Communio* 27, 1 (2000), pp. 171–201.

5. Person, world and history

Two excellent translated essays discuss the crucial topic of the person: Eric de Moulins-Beaufort, 'The Spiritual Man in the Thought of Henri de Lubac', *Communio* 25, 2 (1998), pp. 287–302; and Georges Chantraine, 'Beyond Modernity and Postmodernity: The Thought of Henri de Lubac', *Communio* 17, 2 (1990), pp. 207–219. Rudolf Voderholzer, 'Dogma and History: Henri de Lubac and the Retrieval of Historicity as a Key to Theological Renewal',

Communio 28, 4 (2001), pp. 648–68, is also useful. Two recent and extensive French studies are Vitor Franco Gomes, *Le Paradoxe du désir de Dieu : étude sur le rapport de l'homme à Dieu selon Henri de Lubac* (Études lubaciennes, 4; Paris: Cerf, 2005); and Eric de Moulins-Beaufort, *Anthropologie et mystique selon Henri de Lubac : 'l'esprit de l'homme', ou la présence de Dieu en l'homme* (Études lubaciennes, 3; Paris: Cerf, 2003).

De Lubac's links with Teilhard de Chardin are discussed in Jean-Yves Calvez, *Chrétiens penseurs du social : Maritain, Fessard, Teilhard de Chardin, De Lubac (1920–1940)* (Paris: Cerf, 2002), pp. 137–53; Marc Pelchat, « Pierre Teilhard de Chardin et Henri de Lubac : pour une nouvelle synthèse théologique à l'âge scientifique », *Laval théologique et philosophique* 45 (1989), pp. 255–73; and James R. Pambrun, 'The Presence of God: A Note on the Apologetics of Henri de Lubac and Teilhard de Chardin', *Église et théologie* 10 (1979), pp. 343–68.

6. Faith, belief and reason
Useful articles include Peter Henrici, 'On Mystery in Philosophy', *Communio* 19, 3 (1992), pp. 354–64; and for background Xavier Tilliette, « Le Père de Lubac et le débat de la philosophie chrétienne », *Les Études philosophiques* 1995, 2, « Henri de Lubac et la philosophie », pp. 193–203. The major study is Michel Sales, *L'Être humain et la connaissance naturelle qu'il a de Dieu : essai sur la structure anthropo-théologique fondamentale de la Révélation chrétienne dans la pensée du P. Henri de Lubac* (Paris: Parole et silence, 2003).

7. Christ and the Buddha
The principal study is the collection *L'Intelligence de la rencontre du bouddhisme*, ed. Paul Magnin (Études lubaciennes, 2; Paris: Cerf, 2001). There is little recent or useful work available in English on this topic.

8. Other works
Jean-Pierre Wagner has produced two general expositions in French: *La Théologie fondamentale selon Henri de Lubac* (Paris: Cerf, 1997), and his shorter *Henri de Lubac* (Paris: Cerf, 2001). Antonio Russo's study of Maurice Blondel's impact on de Lubac, *Henri de Lubac : teologia e dogma nella storia. L'influsso di Blondel* (Rome: Studium, 1990) is valuable in understanding de Lubac's philosophical heritage. The same author's *Henri de Lubac : biographie* (Paris: Brepols, 1997) is particularly informative on the social and intellectual context in which his work developed, and includes a useful timeline of his life. An important study of de Lubac's 'dispersed' Christology is Étienne Guibert, *Le Mystère du Christ d'après Henri de Lubac* (Études lubaciennes, 5; Paris: Cerf, 2006).

Bibliography
Karl H. Neufeld and Michel Sales, *Bibliographie Henri de Lubac, S.J. (1925–1970)* (Einsiedeln: Johannes, 1971), lists earlier works and is updated

by « Bibliographie Henri de Lubac, S.J., 1970–1990 », in *Théologie dans l'histoire* (Paris: Desclée, 1990), pp. 408–37, omitted from the English translation TH. Paul McPartlan, *Eucharist Makes the Church*, and Susan Wood, *Spiritual Exegesis and the Church* both include extensive bibliographies which supply material for more recent years. A comprehensive bibliography is projected as vol. 50 of the *Oeuvres complètes*.

INDEX